# LEADERSHIP IS HELL

## HOW TO MANAGE WELL — AND ESCAPE WITH YOUR SOUL

### ROB ASGHAR

Los Angeles
2014

FIGUEROA PRESS
840 Childs Way, 3rd Floor
Los Angeles, CA 90089
Phone: (213) 743-4800
Fax: (213) 743-4804
www.figueroapress.com

Figueroa Press is a division of the USC Bookstore.

Copyright © 2014 by Rob Asghar.
All rights reserved.

Printed in the United States of America

Notice of Rights
All rights reserved. No part of this book may be reproduced or transmitted in any form or by any means, electronic, mechanical, photocopying, recording, or otherwise, without prior written permission from the author, care of Figueroa Press.

Notice of Liability
The information in this book is distributed on an "As is" basis, without warranty. While every precaution has been taken in the preparation of this book, neither the author nor Figueroa nor the USC Bookstore shall have any liability to any person or entity with respect to any loss or damage caused or alleged to be caused directly or indirectly by any text contained in this book.

Figueroa Press and the USC Bookstore are trademarks of the University of Southern California

ISBN-13: 978-0-18-217302-0
ISBN-10: 0-18-217302-X
Library of Congress Control Number: 2014934813

Dedicated to Warren Bennis and Steven Sample, who have given so much to USC and to society as master teacher-practitioners of leadership.

All author royalties will benefit the USC Neighborhood Academic Initiative, launched in 1992 by President Sample, which makes a college education accessible to the next generation of young leaders.

# TABLE OF CONTENTS

| | |
|---|---|
| **ACKNOWLEDGMENTS** | 11 |
| **FOREWORD** | 13 |
| **INTRODUCTION** | 15 |
| **CHAPTER 1: Everyone Knows About Your Achilles' Heel—Except You** | 21 |
|     The Single Biggest Reason Talented People Fail | 22 |
|     Truth Hurts...Then It Heals | 23 |
|     Reality Check | 24 |
|     Joe and Harry Know What You Don't Know | 25 |
|     Jumping Through the Johari Window | 25 |
|     Time to Take Stock | 27 |
|     Why Are You the Last to Know? | 32 |
|         1. Ego | 32 |
|         2. The Polite Entourage | 34 |
|         3. Loyalty | 35 |
|     Building Truthful Organizations and Communities | 36 |
|     Mutual Accountability: Why 360s at the Office Often Fail | 38 |
|     The Achilles Check: Ready, Set...Not Yet...? | 39 |
|         Step 1: Visualize the Worst-Case Scenario | 39 |

| | |
|---|---|
| Step 2: Assemble the Right Sounding Board | 40 |
| Step 3: Choose a Caring Intermediary Who Can Get People Talking | 40 |
| Step 4: Keep Focused on Only Your Achilles' Heel | 44 |
| Step 5: Circle Back and Thank Others | 45 |
| Change and the Serenity Prayer | 45 |
| The Chance to Be a Hero | 46 |
| "I Cannot Do This Alone" | 48 |
| **CHAPTER 2: Your Radar Works Harder Than Your Compass** | **51** |
| The Two-Headed King | 52 |
| What's at Stake? | 54 |
| Six Simple (but Hard) Steps to Charging Up Your Compass | 55 |
| Step 1: Survive the Game of "Simon Says" | 55 |
| Step 2: Tune Out the Comments Section | 56 |
| Step 3: Become Your Own *Best* Critic | 57 |
| Step 4: No More Mr. Nice Guy: Fire Away with Grace | 59 |
| Step 5: No More Mr. Nice Guy, Continued: Fake Some Confidence | 60 |
| Step 6: Channel Your Inner Tiger Mom | 63 |
| Step 7: Manage Your Energy, Not Your Words | 64 |
| Reality Check for the Radar Operator: Why Do I Want to Lead? | 65 |

| | |
|---|---|
| Case Studies in Radaritis | 66 |
|     All Dressed Up with Nowhere to Lead | 66 |
|     Dreaming Worthy Dreams | 68 |
|     Mission Statement Madness | 69 |
|     Success Story: From Radar to a Balanced Radar-Compass | 72 |
| **CHAPTER 3: Your Compass Works Harder Than Your Radar** | **77** |
| Know What You Do | 78 |
| A Certain Amount of Certainty Is *Good* | 79 |
| A Certain Other Amount of Certainty Is *Bad* | 80 |
| Unlike Father, Unlike Son | 81 |
| The Jobs Conundrum | 83 |
| Tuning in to Your Advisers' Frequencies | 84 |
| Better a Team of Rivals than a Team of Parrots | 84 |
| "None of Us Is as Smart as All of Us:" The Practical Case for a Radar | 86 |
| Pericles vs. Plato | 87 |
| The Real Wisdom of the Mob | 88 |
| Cockpit Resource Management | 90 |
| **CHAPTER 4: You Need to Let Go of What You're Not Good At** | **95** |
| Leading Isn't Everything | 96 |
| Reality Check | 98 |
| If You *Must* Lead | 99 |
| Scorsese Leaders: Better Behind the Camera Than in Front of It | 100 |

| | |
|---|---|
| DiCaprio Leaders: Good at the Podium, Bad in the Boardroom | 101 |
| Icarus Leaders: Those Who Make Better Numbers 2s than Number 1s | 102 |
| DiCaprio Leaders = Paper-bag Leaders | 105 |
|     Hiring Duties | 105 |
|     Firing Duties | 108 |
|     Fiscal Duties | 111 |
| **Chapter 5: You're Trying to Prove Yourself, Instead of Just Expressing Yourself** | **113** |
| Cradles of Eminence, Nurseries of Misery | 116 |
| The Obvious Downside to "Never Being Satisfied" | 116 |
| Proving Yourself as a Faustian Bargain: Michael Jordan | 117 |
| Being vs. Doing | 120 |
| R-E-S-P-E-C-T: Find Out What It Means to *You* | 121 |
| The Road to Hell is Paved with a Veneer of Respectability | 122 |
| An Asian Dilemma: Who Writes Your Script? | 122 |
| The Virtue of Being a "Do Nothing" | 123 |
| The Wallenda Factor | 125 |
| Time to Play Ball | 126 |
| Phony Relationships and the Dilemma of Fame | 126 |
| The Bottom Line | 127 |
| No Easy Answers | 128 |

**Chapter 6: You Think, Deep Down, That It Really Might Be All About You** — 131

- Rise and Fall of the Gladstonians — 131
- Gladstonians Won't Prosper for Long in a Disraelian World — 132
- How It Works in Practice — 134
- Clinton vs. Obama vs. Clinton — 135
- Agreeing to Disagree — 137
- A Farewell to Statues — 138
- Moving from Great Monologues to Great Conversations — 138
- Questions for the CEO Interview — 140
- It Takes Two to Get Tangled — 143
- Generation 'N' — 144

**Chapter 7: You Never Can Say Goodbye** — 147

- But What's Next? — 151
- How Do You Know When It's Time to Go — 152
- The Rise and Fall of the Roman Emperor — 152
- Going Home to the Farm — 153
- The American Cincinnatus — 154

**Epilogue: Icarus Fell. No One Noticed.** — **165**

# ACKNOWLEDGMENTS

This book is special to me, in that I see it as a flower that was seeded and nurtured through thousands of hours of wonderful conversations over the years with friends and colleagues—around dinner tables, in boardrooms, at coffeehouses and, of course, in cyber-space—about what leadership truly is.

Without the support and guidance of my editor, Estela Marie Go, this book would have remained a jumble of disconnected thoughts and themes. She deserves the major credit for bringing this project to fruition, and I won't be surprised to see this very talented communicator move soon from behind the scenes to reaching large audiences directly.

USC University Professor Warren Bennis and USC President Emeritus Steve Sample inspired no small portion of the topics and issues that are covered here. These two mentors, with remarkable records as both scholars and practitioners of leadership, have challenged me for years. A generation of students and colleagues has gained immeasurably by working through the complementary philosophies and contrasting approaches of these two giants.

USC President C. L. Max Nikias—a mentor, colleague and one of the most gifted leaders today in any realm—has also been an enormous source of encouragement and wisdom.

As a collaborator and counselor, USC chaplain and religious life dean Varun Soni has been a godsend—or more appropriately, a Vishnu-send, given that he is the first Hindu to serve as a chaplain at a major American university. He and his wife Shakti Nadoo have been among the most important influences in my life in recent years.

Debra Ono, aside from embodying the qualities of character that this book tries to illuminate and champion, was of immense assistance in the final phases of this book. So too was Lorynne Young.

I thank my family and hope this book may someday be of value to my nephews Nicholas and Zain and my nieces Emaan, Zara and Natalie—all five being astonishingly gifted persons with enormous contributions to make to this world that they've inherited.

I thank Tiffany Quon and Rhonda Bonstein of USC's Figueroa Press for their terrific guidance and assistance throughout this project. And finally, I thank the many people who have made the conversation around the table so compelling over the years—my Forbes editor Frederick Allen, Elisa Schreiber, Andrew Whitelock, Lori Putnam, Tim Chambers, Dan Cray, Martha Harris, Christian Camozzi, Marie Domingo, Laura Galloway, Ben Malcolmson, Ann and Mickey Corcoran, Joanne and Eric Weidman, Laura Harbert, Dale Bruner, Steve Norris, Kevin Ramon, Tim Knight, Jessica del Mundo, Julie Sweeney, Robin Romans and so many other dear friends and colleagues.

**Rob Asghar**
**March 2014**

# FOREWORD

As the dean of religious life at the University of Southern California, I'm frequently asked by bright and ambitious young people to discuss concepts such as leadership and success. As students with better-than–4.0 grade point averages and near-perfect SAT scores, they come to campus knowing they've been placed on a fast track for success by their parents, teachers, and community. But they long to know more deeply what meaningful success is—and particularly what it might look like in their personal contexts. This search for meaning, purpose, identity, and authenticity is not unique for today's university students, but rather it is a shared aspiration for all of us. Indeed, this search is deeply spiritual and fundamentally human at its core.

As a way of understanding organizational dynamics and explaining leadership principles, Rob Asghar juxtaposes the central tenets of both Western and Eastern spiritual traditions with contemporary leadership models, styles, and examples. In doing so, Asghar points us to a new type of leadership that is inspired by the timeless wisdom of the world's enduring spiritual and philosophical traditions. Such ethical leadership is predicated on wrestling with one's ego while knowing when to engage and when to renounce.

Rob Asghar's major contribution to the growing body of leadership literature is his challenge for thoughtful people to define leadership in a manner that is authentic to them. For some, this may involve letting go of traditional markers of success and achievement. Indeed, as Asghar reminds us, many talented persons can make their most beneficial impact without assuming the burdens of conventional management. For those who do hear and respond to the call to be managers and conventional leaders of organizations and causes, this book is a manual for how to do it well. It explores the complex Faustian bargains involved in high-stakes leadership and in pursuing other kinds of celebrity and fame. And most importantly, it offers a way to finish the job without losing one's soul.

Good leaders cultivate passion and purpose in their lives, and transform themselves while transforming their organizations. They conscientiously combine an internal moral compass with an external awareness of their stakeholders' talents and needs. They are deeply invested in meaning and authenticity, and in proactively liberating themselves from traditional definitions of success and achievement. And even though they understand that leadership is hell, they empower themselves to embrace and enjoy the fleeting moments of heaven.

**Varun Soni**
**March 2014**

# INTRODUCTION

Imagine the following conversation with a 10-year-old:

> "What do you want to be when you grow up?"
> "In charge."
> "Excuse me?"
> "I want to be in charge. I want to run things."
> "What exactly do you want to be in charge of?"
> "Whatever. Something. Anything."

Then we pat her on the head, sign her up for leadership boot camp, and convince her that she is the secret to our society's future.

No one says, "I want to be a follower. I don't much care what area it is, so long as I'm following someone else." And certainly no one writes books helping such a person to be an effective follower. Today, *everyone* needs to be a leader.

But is leadership a Faustian bargain? Too often it is. Most leadership experts play off your ego. Few actually help shape your ego, which must be neither too large nor too small in order to manage effectively and to get out with your soul intact. That's where this book is different.

This book will offer you some of the most important leadership advice you will ever receive. But to be able to receive it, you need first to admit something: Leadership is *hell*.

Leadership looks like paradise from the outside and Hades from within. Like parenting, it looks romantic when one is not immersed up to her elbows in soiled diapers.

Leadership is a headache, that most thankless of jobs, because in most cases they will only build a statue of you after you're dead, which is when they begin feeling some mix of nostalgia and guilt.

Yet because the human need to "be somebody" is so powerful and universal, leadership and management training happens to be a global industry, to the tune of $60 billion a year. I know this. I've been a part of it, sometimes behind the scenes and other times behind the microphone.

**Leggo My Ego**

Your ego can be your best friend, but often it's your worst enemy. You can't stand up and make a difference without having a strong sense of self. You can't move in a new direction without having a solid ego.

But when that ego gets overinflated by one pound per square inch, you risk blowing out a tire or racing off a cliff. When you become a leader, every circumstance you face will be one that tends to overinflate your ego and set you up for failure.

This book will take you on a journey, allowing you to look over the rails and down at famous leaders, ranging from Caesar in antiquity to Joe Paterno in our time, who got it wrong and who paid awful prices. But it will also show you leaders who got it right—people ranging from Cincinnatus to John Wooden who didn't go too far and who didn't get swallowed whole by ego and the false prerogatives of leadership. You'll see seven roads to hell within the world of management—and seven roads out of hell, to guide you to safety.

Here's what those roads look like:

**Road Number 1: You have blind spots that keep you from succeeding.** You're the only person in the room who isn't aware of your Achilles' heel that will keep you from realizing your dreams. **You now need to make office backstabbing work for you, not against you, by getting a 360-degree view that will allow you to discover and overcome your blind spots.**

**Road Number 2: Your radar is working harder than your compass.** You're the sort of person who can walk into a situation and can read other people's feelings. You want everyone to be happy—more importantly, you want them to be happy with *you*. You get derailed easily, changing your mind and your direction in the face of any resistance. **You now need to learn how to find your own true north, and to bring that to your leadership efforts.**

**Road Number 3: Your compass is working harder than your radar.** You're trampling others on your way to your goals. You have certainty about your direction—just like all those other people who raced off cliffs on their quest for the stars. **You now need to learn how to interpret other people's hopes, in order to find a direction in which you can all move at the same speed.**

**Road Number 4: You need to let go of what you're not good at.** You may be charismatic, you may enjoy attention, and many people may enjoy you—but you may still be a mediocre manager, unskilled at follow-through, handling budgets or making tough decisions. Conversely, you may be great at the behind-the-scenes work, but you'll never be the charming face of the organization. **You now need to admit that it's time to let some things go and hand them to others who can manage better.**

**Road Number 5: You're trying to prove yourself, instead of just expressing yourself.** Because you're on a desperate quest for respect, you don't know the Zen of playfully getting lost in what you love, without regard for outcomes. **You now need to give yourself permission to *do* the things you love to do instead of trying to become the lofty figure you'd love to *be*.**

**Road Number 6: You'd never admit it, but you still secretly think that it just might be all about you.** You see leadership as your best chance to put the spotlight on yourself. **You now need to discover how much more you'll be appreciated by placing that spotlight on those around you.**

**Road Number 7: You never can say goodbye.** Like Julius Caesar (or Joe Paterno), you risk damaging your legacy by staying on too long. **You now need to find your inner Cincinnatus and discover the virtue of walking away at the right time.**

This book is here to help you find the right balance for your own life. In some cases, it will challenge you to develop a stronger sense of self. In other cases, it will help you distinguish between what you're all about at your core and what you falsely believe you must achieve due to pressures that others may have placed on you (or on imaginary pressures that exist only in the insecure parts of your mind).

In whatever case, you'll learn the best way to make an impact that's an authentic expression of who you are and what you're about. This book will give you the chance to do what 95 percent of human beings who walked this earth never got a chance to do: To live your own life.

It's not easy to navigate the cliffs and curves of leadership—it requires honesty, from yourself and from others. It will take many hours of self-reflection and willingness to receive feedback from friends, family and colleagues. But it will make all the difference. In the process, your career, your relationships and your legacy will be transformed.

20　Leadership is Hell

# ONE

## EVERYONE KNOWS ABOUT YOUR ACHILLES' HEEL—EXCEPT YOU

**THE ROAD TO HELL:** You're the only person in the room who isn't aware of that fatal flaw that will keep you from your dreams. Everyone else is quite familiar with it, as they talk regularly about how you talk too much or take no prisoners or quit too easily or are unreliable. But they're not planning to tell you because it's easier to talk about your flaws behind your back than to your face—and they fear that you might hate them or hurt them if you knew what they all thought. In short, you don't know how to make backstabbing work for you instead of against you.

**THE ROAD OUT OF HELL:** You are able to solicit an authentic, brutally honest 360-view of yourself, courtesy of colleagues, friends, family and, whenever possible, a skilled shrink. Caution: This is not for the faint of heart. You should hold off on such life-transforming feedback until you are truly ready for it (in other words, after you're confident you can follow through on your promise not to passive-aggressively bludgeon others with silent contempt after they give you their honest perspective).

## The Single Biggest Reason Talented People Fail

Many gifted, intelligent, charming, decent, charitable and hard-working people fail. One should go so far as to say that most such people fall short of their dreams or at least their potential, because of one reason: They failed to identify in themselves an Achilles' heel that was common knowledge to other people.

If they had been bold enough to look for that Achilles' heel, they would have succeeded.

Achilles was one of the mighty Trojans' greatest warriors. His mother Thetis attempted to give him immortality by dipping him in the river Styx. She ended up making him 99 percent immortal and one percent tragic figure, because he indeed became immortal—except in the heel that remained in his mother's hand while she immersed him in the flowing waters, the heel through which he would receive a minor but *fatal* wound.

Some people get negative feedback that they didn't solicit. Quarterbacks get booed and aspiring singers get laughed off stage by the judges of televised variety shows. But for most of us, it's hard to get candid feedback about what constitutes an Achilles' heel that must be remedied or at least protected. We don't know how to find out where our blind spots are or when we might be at greatest risk for running off a cliff during our race to the mountaintop.

- This explains why so many consultants are stunned when they're fired, blaming their setback on their clients' fickleness or duplicity.
- This explains why so many bright young people can't get their careers on a meaningful track, blaming their fate on a bad economy or the inability of older managers to "get" the work-life balance of a new generation.

- This explains why so many middle managers stagnate halfway up the ladder, blaming their superiors for being selfish or dumb.
- This explains why so many talented entrepreneurs fail in the early stages of a new venture.
- This explains why even legendary leaders eventually run out of luck and face the ultimate indignity—living long enough to see their reputation and legacy evaporate.

**Truth Hurts...Then It Heals**

All along, their peers may have been talking about their Achilles' heel. Today, your peers, friends and family may be discussing yours.

Why don't they tell you? Because they're being polite and a little cowardly. They may feel terrible about it because they know their politeness and cowardice may yet spoil your career, as you charge out into battle, oblivious to your own Achilles' heel. But if you truly seek to realize your full potential, you have no choice but to do a frightfully honest self-assessment. You need to actively invite, even demand, rigorous candor from your friends, associates and family, *so they can help you identify the dangerous blind spot or Achilles' heel that you never identify on your own.*

A wise man said, "Everyone thinks he's a good driver, a good joke-teller and a good listener." Of course, we know that half of the people out there are by statistical necessity below average at those activities. (Worse yet, many of the people who are in positions that require them to be good listeners turn out to be lousy listeners!)

While there are reasons that most leaders and would-be leaders fall short of their ambitions, they are highly fixable. In this chapter, we'll look at:

1. How to be honest with yourself about whether you're ready to receive brutal but constructive feedback that can save or enhance your career.
2. How to round up a good "jury"—the right mix of people who care enough to be honest and constructive about whether you have one particular blind spot or Achilles' heel.
3. Why you should find someone who can interview these people on your behalf.
4. Why you should be interested in *only* the common threads that emerge from your intermediary's conversations with the interviewees.
5. How to take responsibility and take your next steps forward.

**Reality Check**

Psychologists have known for years that human beings have a hard time coming up with a clear view of themselves. Some are too humble; most are too arrogant. Many times people are overly humble or overly arrogant at precisely the wrong moments.

Studies routinely show that six out of 10 people believe they're above average. I suspect it means that a few above-average people rate themselves *below* average—while a higher number of below-average people cheerfully rate themselves *above* average.

Another study some years ago showed that two-thirds of people believed that most other people are selfish—yet only one in six people believed that he or she was selfish! Obviously, the numbers don't add up. We're better at seeing the speck in another's eye than a log in our own eye, to use the old Biblical proverb.

## Joe and Harry Know What *You* Don't Know

The issue of blind spots and Achilles' heels can be understood through something called the Johari Window. Some 60 years ago, Joseph Luft and Harry Ingham created a simple visual model to understand how each of us interacts within our organization. They believed it offered a model for overcoming problems in how we interact.

The window is a simple square divided into four sections, each one depicting some aspect of what we know and don't know about ourselves.

|  | Known to Self | *Not* Known to Self |
|---|---|---|
| Known by Others | ARENA | BLIND SPOT |
| *Not* Known by Others | FACADE | UNKNOWN |

## Jumping Through the Johari Window

At the top left, the ARENA quad represents what everyone knows about you—it's the public arena in which you live and operate. For instance, you love to wear blue, and you work on Washington Boulevard—and this is not news to you or to anyone else.

Moving clockwise, the BLIND SPOT quad represents what's known by others but not by you. For instance, you have spinach in your teeth but you insist on smiling broadly all day anyway. Or you don't realize that everyone else is cheering for someone else to get promoted ahead of you because of some past actions of yours that may have been unintentional or misunderstood.

The UNKNOWN quad represents those things that neither you nor others notice. For instance, Enron chairman Ken Lay, at the top of his game, had convinced himself, his employees, the media and public that he was a stellar and trustworthy businessman.

The FACADE quad represents that part of you that you intentionally keep hidden from others.

The Johari model suggests that you and your company or family or bridge club become stronger as you increase open communication between yourself and others regarding those four quads. Trust is built when you're able to hear from others about your blind spots, when you're able to let down your own guard, and when you're willing to help others see past their own blind spots.

Marshall Goldsmith, one of the world's best executive coaches, compares most business executives to golfers: They both tend to be blissfully unaware of their weakenessess, and thus they fail to shore up those weakenesses.


While we speak of blind spots, a more helpful image involves unpleasant smells. Researchers at the air freshener-maker Febreze found some years ago that people who most needed their product were least likely to realize they needed the product because they'd grown accustomed to the smell of cat litter in their homes or stale french fries in their car seats. The smells became invisible to their nostrils while everyone else could smell the stench.

Scientists have found that we can grow accustomed rapidly to offensive smells in our midst: Within minutes, we can become accustomed to odors ranging from rotten cabbage to bad breath.

In much the same way, we have quirks that may sabotage us in ways that we can't realize because we've either grown accustomed to them or because identifying them is as hard as identifying a defect in the very retina that we use to perceive things.

Sure, the imagery may seem harsh. No one likes to believe they "stink," even in just one area of life. Leaders and would-be leaders in particular have at least a strain of narcissism that makes them believe that they sweat rose petals at worst.

There are two primary ways in which this derails careers in management and leadership. You're weak in some key aspect of your craft, but you don't know it. Or you're weak at the political and social aspects of your career, but you don't know it.

**Time to Take Stock**

Be honest about your own life as a manager or aspiring leader.

- Have you plateaued in your career? Are you not rising at the rate you're accustomed to?
- Do you fear that other people don't "get" how brilliant or hardworking or clever you are?
- Do you feel puzzled or frustrated, as though something is holding you back from the kind of success that you feel you deserve?
- Are your actions having the reaction you intended? If not, there may be other actions you are taking that are having unintended reactions and consequences.

If you answered "yes" to any of these questions, the drag and inertia in your career may be attributable to a fault of yours that others are reacting to, unbeknownst to you.

Goldsmith, who has coached thousands of executives to find and fix their blind spots, offers a tantalizing and counterintuitive notion: Many people plateau in their careers because the very traits that help them achieve a certain degree of success end up preventing them from having further success (thus came the title of his book, *What Got You Here Won't Get You There: How Successful People Become Even More Successful*).

In short, a virtue may become an Achilles' heel over time, such as when a person's stubbornness helps her reach one level of success then ruins her when she doubles down on it while trying to reach the next level of success. Saying, "That's who I am, it's gotten me this far, so I won't change" is a fool's game.

Yet many other times, a person has a blind spot that she is able to overcome for a while, due to fortuitous alignment of the stars and planets or the guidance and affection of others. But the person sputters out or falls off a cliff when fortune and friends can't keep her on a steady course.

Let's look at some categories and examples of Achilles' heels in management and leadership.

### 1. "I'm starting to get annoying."

**Sophia hogs the oxygen.** She has to say something about everything. Some people find it charming, and they're willing to encourage her. Others find it grating, but they bite their tongue. Eventually the less-amused colleagues begin leaving her out of meetings because they have a full agenda and frankly don't have the time for her stories, her sidebars, her jokes and her issues. She realizes others are having meetings or making decisions without consulting her, and she feels betrayed and demoralized.

**Zoe feels let down by the people that she's let down.** She's whip-smart, and she knows what it would take to conquer the world. She generates brilliant ideas that get people excited. But then she gets too distracted to bring any of her ideas to fruition. In a recurring scenario, people excitedly offer their support and their desire to partner with her, but inevitably, they quietly withdraw their support and stop taking her calls. Like Sophia, she feels frustrated and betrayed.

## 2. "I have no idea how bad I am at this."

**Logan thinks he has great excuses for ignoring his superiors' orders.** He believes he's utterly brilliant. Yet while he can be brilliant, in fits and spurts, he's not as talented as he imagines, and this has set him up for failure. He does get some feedback from management that's quite clear and would be quite helpful, but he's decided that those above him tragically don't "get it." When he then gets a negative performance review, he feels persecuted and misunderstood.

**Aiden isn't as good behind the camera as he is in front of it.** This CEO is charming and can sound visionary to employees and to reporters. He's been on CNN and has wowed viewers, speaking about long-term opportunities in his industry. But he's mediocre at managing budgets, making difficult decisions, inspiring and correcting his direct reports, and all the "diaper changing" that is the domain of the true leader.

**Madison isn't as good in front of the camera as she is behind it.** This company president loves to give long and frequent speeches with her trademark stories, but speaking isn't her strength; managing shrewdly and diplomatically behind the scenes is where her political genius comes out.

**Ava thinks her colleagues are incompetent but doesn't realize how she herself is disorganized.** Ava is similar to Zoe in an earlier scenario. She is extraordinarily smart and strategic. She's running behind on organizing the big event, but she has enough confidence in herself to figure that it'll go well anyway. No, she didn't return your call, but who nowadays makes phone calls? No, she didn't return your email either, but you have to understand that she gets hundreds of those per hour. And yet Ava wonders why a bright light such as she hasn't been promoted as quickly as the dimmer wits in her vicinity.

**3. "My spine is still in the shop."**

**Hannah is quick to protect weak employees under her.** Some of her lieutenants have reputations as underachievers, but Hannah knows that these employees have great potential—along with real challenges that they are boldly navigating in their personal lives. She repeatedly lobbies for them, and she believes she is doing the right thing ethically by championing them against naysayers. She begins to worry about her own job security.

**Connor is full of large ambitions, but he is pulled by everyone else's agenda.** Three years after assuming a management role with great promise, he hasn't delivered. He asks everyone for more time, but he can sense that he may be running out of it.

**Matthew doesn't know what to do now that he's seated at the adults' table.** He worked slavishly and skillfully to work his way up and earn a space in the C-suite. But his mindset is still that of someone used to deferring to others. He believes that his title should automatically result in others giving him more respect, and he doesn't do enough to earn that respect. He's seated among leaders, but he won't be viewed as their peer until he begins acting the part.

**Ryan is a victim of circumstances.** He blames the board chairman, the economy, the ex-wife, and the myriad conspiracies for the difficulties he faces at the office. The idea that he may be the common denominator in his troubles has yet to dawn on him.

**4. "I'm not aware how long my list of potential assassins is."**

**Brooke is the Terminator.** She is the smartest person in the room. She knows what needs to get done and knows the direction in which she needs to go. But she tramples a good number of bystanders, potential allies and former allies along the way. She feels she's making good progress, but she doesn't realize the extent to which others are conspiring to throw up roadblocks, if only to keep themselves from the threat of becoming road kill.

**Cole is the Company Cassandra.** He's more realistic than everyone else. He knows the company's sales objective is overoptimistic, even impossible. He's tried to tell this to anyone who will listen; and he can tell that, increasingly, no one is listening. His jeremiads fail to draw the attention he feels they should. He feels like a martyr being dragged off by the mob to a messy conclusion, against his will and better judgment.

**Debra is in your face.** All the time. She wears loud colors and has loud opinions. She's not always wrong, but she's always at war. Others begin to lock her out of the decision-making process.

In all these cases, a common denominator exists: the manager or would-be leader with the Achilles' heel tends to feel disrespected and underappreciated—never realizing that the lack of appreciation has to do with his Achilles' heel, not others' lack of taste or decency.

Some of these examples are important enough to be further examined in later chapters.

**Why Are You the Last to Know?**

We need to understand the three reasons that we have dangerous blind spots and unknown weaknesses:

1. our own egos,
2. our polite entourage, and
3. the "loyalty bind" that exists in most organizations.

**1. Ego**

Ego is an overriding factor. A recurring theme in this book is that too little ego will make for a weak leader and too much ego will make for a disastrous one. The leader's challenge is to find that sweet spot, that Goldilocks Zone of the "just right" amount of ego to allow herself to move forward with confidence, without charging off a cliff.

A person goes to church or temple and hears a sermon about how all pride and vanity and ego are bad. The same person goes to a management seminar and hears about how leadership requires an appalling amount of self-confidence and certainty. The Goldilocks zone of ego, for leaders, is a mysterious place, one that's hard to locate and very hard to inhabit for the long haul.

Ego is what allows Sophia to believe that she is more interesting than she is, which then leads her to dominate discussions. It's not that she is completely oblivious to the reactions of others. Some people find her charming and give her positive feedback, and that allows her then to blind herself to even the possibility that they represent a minority view.

Ego is what makes Madison overdo her public role. Frankly, she's a better director than actor, and should be behind the camera, not in front of it. By making herself too visible within her organization, she loses some mystique and respect. But she struggles to let go of the public role, because she feels that it's a key perk of the job she worked so hard to earn.

Aiden, by contrast, is a better actor than director. But his ego pushes him not just to be on stage, but to be at the center of all decision-making processes even though his tendency is to clog up those processes as a human bottleneck.

You see what we could do, right? Madison and Aiden could join forces at one of their companies, with him handling most public roles and her managing most boardroom roles. In that way, both keep their pride from allowing them to overstep into areas where they are weak.

Matthew, for his part, has enough ego to want a seat at the table and enough ego to feel he deserves the respect of others. But he lacks the ego to give himself permission to lead, initiate and drive the vision and mission of the organization.

Brooke, Cole and Debra all suffer from a know-it-all attitude. They don't play well in the sandbox because they believe they uniquely have all the answers. Their confidence can be enormous assets—if they learn when to dial it back.

## 2. The Polite Entourage

In human society, backbiting happens. Your challenge is to make backbiting work *for* you, not against you.

Your friends and family have been talking openly about your shortcomings, but they didn't tell you. What kinds of friends or family are they? The truth is that they're just like most everyone else: They're built for polite society, and they can't speak to you as easily as they can speak about you behind your back. Admit that you're as guilty of this as anybody else.

We love to mock people behind their back, but most of us would frankly be unable to criticize Attila the Hun to his face if the opportunity presented itself.

The reality is that insincerity is that force that holds society together. Ambrose Bierce defined politeness as "the most respectable hypocrisy." Indeed, many marriages endured solely because one spouse told another, "No, those pants don't at all make you look fat."

If everyone said to everyone else's face what they really believed, there would be no end to our griefs and no relief from our woes. No one would leave his house, except to avenge slights. We know this in our bones and it's why we are accustomed to hold our tongue.


Giving people permission to speak candidly is crucial. But know that just giving that permission won't automatically create candor. People are too conditioned to be candid only when you're not around. (As we'll see, this is a reason to draft a trusted colleague or friend to get candid feedback from others on your behalf.)

As a frequent public speaker who spent some time on the professional circuit, I found an intriguing pattern a few years ago. If someone told me, "You did a *great* job up there," that usually meant they thought I'd done "a good job." If they said, "*Good* job, Rob," that meant "Fair enough job, Rob." If they just shook their head awkwardly and said with a forced smile, "Thank you for sharing," that meant, "Let's put this incident behind us and not speak of it any further."

The challenge for me was to use other people's feedback strategically, not just to puff me up. I learned to seek people's flattery less than their concrete observations about whether my key points seemed to "land" with the audience or whether the flow of my presentation was as effective as it could be. Once they know I'm sincere about wanting to improve, they become more willing to say, "Here's what you could do better."

### 3. Loyalty

Oftentimes the people around you are too polite to say the truth about you. But many times the people around you are too loyal to see the truth about you. This is what psychologists refer to as the "loyalty bind." Glaring examples include the child-abuse scandals at Penn State University and within the Roman Catholic Church. In both cases, it wasn't merely people at the top who refused to see the truth—it was the faithful flocks who attempted to shame or intimidate those who would dare question their beloved leaders.

This is hardly the first book to warn leaders not to live in a bubble, or not to surround themselves with overly deferential followers. The challenge is to acknowledge how talk in this area is cheap.

A CEO often gave lectures on the leadership lessons he'd learned. He would sometimes observe, "It's essential for a leader *not* to surround himself with yes men. But it's so easy for a leader to do so."

As I recall, most of his aides would respond to that line with enthusiastic nods and by gushing, "Yes, yes, that's a really powerful point, sir."

And there you have it.

As a leader, you have to have an almost infinite love for your organization or your cause to be able to find advisers who won't simply parrot your views. The parroting isn't necessarily a consequence of their selfishness or their desire for self-preservation. It's because of the "loyalty bind," which gives them an exaggerated view of your effectiveness.

## Building Truthful Organizations and Communities

While insincerity has its social value, by allowing a veneer of politeness to mask potentially hurtful sentiments, it famously results in codependent communities and organizations.

"The less justified a man is in claiming excellence for his own self, the more ready he is to claim all excellence for his nation, his religion, his race or his holy cause," the philosopher Eric Hoffer wrote in his landmark 1951 book, *The True Believer*.

For a person to make such a claim on behalf of a tribe with which he affiliates requires unwavering loyalty. Loyalty, as noted earlier, is a form of pride and ego. It is often a collective pride in our connection to an organization or nation or religion or holy cause or sports team.

Loyalty often comes at the cost of the ability to see reality clearly. Yet whatever one's values and loyalties are, we all want to be able to see the world as it really is. "To see what is in front of one's nose needs a constant struggle," George Orwell observed. We all know there's a difference between the romanticism of an adolescent schoolgirl and the cool-headed realism of a 60-year-old woman, and there's a proportional difference between each one's ability to view life as it is.

Of all the various kinds of organizations and causes, the loyalty bind may be most pernicious in philanthropic and nonprofit institutions. Such organizations are filled with people who usually are more driven by ideals than by money.

They lionize their leaders, who often serve as proud symbols of their institution's goodness. They bask in that glory and become loathe to disrupt the positive energy. It allows Penn State constituents to subconsciously hold their own brotherhood above the interests of others. It doesn't intentionally forgive or overlook crimes against innocent children, but it rationalizes them away while seeking to express perfect loyalty.

In the case of religious institutions, there is a predisposition to see the leader as a proxy for divine authority. I watched a historic church—which was the largest Protestant congregation in North America in its heyday—crumble to within an inch of its life as a bumbling pastor overspent and under-planned, continually convincing the bulk of his flock and his lay leaders that "God demands our faithful obedience, even though we don't know yet where He is taking us." It took bold persons at that church to stand up to the pastor and to his well-meaning followers to initiate a messy divorce that was finally brought about by a denominational governing board. The church survived because of their boldness and their willingness to perform a thankless task of honesty.

Yet the pastor himself may well have been successful, for his own sake and his organization's sake, if he'd been willing to heed their cautions earlier.

## Mutual Accountability: Why 360s at the Office Often Fail

By some accounts, half of American organizations use some form of 360-style processes in their performance evaluations. Often, the results are lacking, which is one reason we have yet to achieve organizational nirvana.

The Gallup Organization famously does a modified 360 of sorts—a Q12 process that asks employees 12 questions that help determine how "engaged" they are in their workplace. (The questions relate to whether an employee feels appreciated, feels able to make a valued contribution, is supported by colleagues, and other such factors.) The more engaged the employees are, Gallup says, the more productive they are and the stronger the organization.

Gallup further links each employee's engagement to the quality of management that she receives from her immediate supervisor. I coordinated a Q12 process with Gallup representatives at a publicly held company with 1,800 employees several years ago and found the exercise to be helpful...to a point.

The exercise can produce some helpful insights and multi-perspectived comparisons of the effectiveness of managers. But a manager may keep employees reasonably engaged yet suffer from a blind spot nonetheless, and the straightforwardness of the Gallup method is not designed to address that.

The main reason that 360 processes fail to improve workplaces (and leaders) as much as they should is that they are often used sparingly within an organization. Sometimes a top manager will make a subordinate manager or other employee go through the process, without going through the process herself.

This violates the goal of making a 360 into a constructive process and can even make it destructive. Others are free to vent aggressively, knowing they won't themselves be held to such scrutiny. The subject in such a process can become the victim of dogpiling by his peers.

Yet while awaiting the perfect 360 process to arrive at your own organization, and to be administered properly thoughout the organization, you can take some crucial action yourself.

### The Achilles Check: Ready, Set... Not Yet...?

A 360-degree review can be life-changing and career-transforming, and you can undertake one yourself... unless you're not ready for it, in which case it might wreck your relationships and sabotage your self-esteem.

"Can you drink from this cup?" Jesus once asked two followers who thought themselves readier than they really were for a challenging assignment. You need a 360 review, but don't get it before you're ready for it. Here are some suggestions on how to sense if you're ready.

### Step 1: Visualize the Worst-Case Scenario

Play it out first in your head. If you ask a friend or colleague the equivalent of a "Do these pants make me look fat?" question, can you honestly deal with an unpleasantly honest response? You owe it to them to not double-cross them by asking them for more candor than you can cope with.

If you can visualize yourself graciously receiving and productively utilizing even the harshest feedback, you're ready enough to go. But if you have even a modest suspicion that you may struggle to look the deliverer of bad news in the eye at the next cocktail party, do yourself and him a favor and postpone the truth-seeking until you're readier for it.

Make yourself readier for it by being mindful of how even feedback that could seem humiliating at first can be liberating at last.

## Step 2: Assemble the Right Sounding Board

Like most managers, you likely are surrounded by a mix of people—sensitive people who couldn't be paid to tell you how they really feel; congenitally supportive mother-hen types who feel you can do no wrong; and caustic critics who always feel you have a little too much room for improvement.

You may have already realized that your own family may play all these roles splendidly at the Thanksgiving table, but you nevertheless want a mix of work colleagues, acquaintances and intimates.

How many people? That depends. Goldsmith will speak, separately, to an average of 15 persons when he's brought in to assess how and where an executive might improve. He will speak to your superiors, your peers, your underlings and, oftentimes, your family.

But Goldsmith is usually looking for a more comprehensive set of data about the executives than you necessarily need. For your purposes, you can do the job with separate conversations with as few as five people.

## Step 3: Choose a Caring Intermediary Who Can Get People Talking

Remember your mission here: To make backbiting work for you, not against you. Because people find it so much easier to talk about your foibles when you're

Leadership is Hell    41

not in the room, in at least some cases you would do well to find an advocate or intermediary to stimulate the discussion without you around, and then report back to you.

Such an intermediary has to be an exceptional person—one who has your best interests at heart, and who wouldn't turn the project into his or her personal mission to remold you according to his or her personal preferences.

The intermediary also has to have enough integrity to resist turning the soliciting of feedback into an opportunity to "out" colleagues who gave harsh feedback.

Approach possible sounding board members to tell them you'd like their help in taking the next step forward in your career, and that you'd love their honest feedback. Tell them that you don't need them to give you the feedback directly. They would be giving the feedback to your intermediary (by telephone or in person, or possibly by email, fax machine or carrier pigeon).

They should feel no pressure to be a part of the exercise. No one person, whether a boss or subordinate or friend or spouse, is crucial for this process. After all, if you have a true Achilles' heel that demands your attention, it will be apparent to many people who've known you over the years. There will always be enough people to give you a critical mass of feedback.

### Step 4: Keep Focused on Only Your Achilles' Heel

**You don't need a complete audit of everything that people would change about you.** That would confuse and overwhelm even the most insensitive and ruthless despot. Stalin would have stayed at home, crying in bed (while having everyone else exiled to

Siberia, of course.) Rather, you just need to identify *whether* you have an Achilles' heel that needs to be addressed.

In Chapter 2, we'll explore in greater depth how to listen to the counsel of others without being pulled excessively by the force of their counsel. It is crucial that you not take all criticisms at face value.

Screenwriters and novelists spend much of their time soliciting the opinions of others. "Here's my manuscript—can you give me your 'notes' sometime soon?" they say. You now have to take their literary baby into your arms and figure how to balance candor with a desire to maintain your friendship.

A screenwriter friend once told me that he found it helpful to follow a certain procedure in soliciting feedback.

He would give his manuscript to three different friends and colleagues and would encourage them to be brutally honest. But if one person criticized an aspect of his story, he didn't worry—he figured that just reflected an idiosyncrasy of that person. If two people criticized that same aspect, he'd consider carefully what he was hearing. And if all three criticized it, he knew he had an issue to deal with.

That approach works well for an Achilles check. Not every criticism of you reflects an Achilles' heel, and you shouldn't respond to every concern that others have about you. Some people will like how loud you are in the morning, and others will find it tiresome. Your real challenge is to find where the feedback "lines up"—where the pattern indicates a clear sense that your approach needs to be changed.

In that spirit, tell the sounding board members that your intermediary has been instructed to keep their particular responses confidential: They should know that the intermediary will only report back common threads and recurring themes, rather than any one person's nitpicking or negativity.

Give the intermediary the names of colleagues, friends and family members who are willing to offer candid but constructive feedback.

I mentioned earlier that at many companies, 360 processes are given only selectively, which results in some people who aren't under evaluation to savage those who are under evaluation. The same effect can happen, to a degree, in the Achilles check.

Goldsmith notes that, in his own assessments, he asks sounding board members if they would be willing to commit to changing something in themselves for the better. That act of commitment can help ensure that interviewees bring the healthiest mindset to this small matter of your professional future. You and your intermediary may find this to be useful.

The process works well when the intermediary first asks the interviewee to talk about your distinct strengths. That allows the interviewee to warm up and get into a positive and constructive frame of mind. The intermediary should assure the interviewee that this is not intended to be an exhaustive inventory of your personality—it is simply an exercise that helps identify if and whether you need to address some aspect of your life. Then, the intermediary shifts to whether the interviewee can identify weaknesses on your part that *can be remedied*—shortcomings that *can be changed*.

Here are some statements and questions that the intermediary can employ, using "Bob" as a generic subject of the exercise:

1. What do you consider to be Bob's strengths?

2. Does Bob have a blind spot—a weakness that he may not be aware of but which you suspect many other people are aware of?
3. Please finish this sentence: "Bob would be more successful in his career if_____."

That's it. Three simple questions are sufficient to do the job. Now it's the intermediary's job to deliver the common, recurring information that he or she received, while keeping full confidence regarding who said what.

I underwent the process myself a while ago, using my trusted friend Estela as an intermediary, and a sounding board consisting of one current colleague who knows me well; three past colleagues, all of whom have known me well over a considerable part of my career; and one of my brothers.

The unexpected—yet not too surprising—outcome was that my Achilles' heel was to complain more readily than I'll take action to fix what's wrong. After briefly complaining about what a flawed process it was, and why I need higher-quality colleagues and family members, I took the advice to heart and recognized it as a gift. I may have suspected that this tendency was one of my weaknesses, but until then I didn't necessarily believe that others close to me had noticed it and identified it as my Achilles' heel.

Depending on one's perspective, that could seem a minor flaw or a fatal one. But that's the piercing point of the Achilles myth: It's the little weaknesses that do you in. For myself, the feedback was pivotal as I moved from the mid-career stage to the crucial next one. It forced me to see myself as the prime mover in my life, rather than someone who might wait passively for an opportunity. In short it confirmed that, in many cases, I had an underinflated ego. (Although most leadership blind spots involve overinflated egos, the next chapter will examine the underinflation tendency in particular depth.)

## Step 5: Circle Back and Thank Others

Once you've gotten a sense of how others assess your chief weakness, you don't need to stop there.

You can share the results of the exercise with your sounding board and thank them. Some will then be eager to speak candidly about their own perspective—if you can assure them that they are safe to do so. You have to promise not to hold their candor against them in the future, which can be harder than it may seem.

## Change and the Serenity Prayer

The challenge is always to stay positive and constructive, and to be oblivious to the rest. The Serenity Prayer, first uttered by the theologian Reinhold Niebuhr and made famous by 12 Steps programs, goes, "God, grant me the serenity to accept the things I cannot change, the courage to change the things I can, and the wisdom to know the difference."

This is critical. For instance, I happen to be a compact 5'7". One good friend once told me, "Oh, Rob, you'd be a more commanding leader if only you were a foot taller."

The next time I gave a presentation, I stood on two phone directories for the first minute. Then I kicked the phone directories aside and moved on with my life. There's nothing I can do about my height except be happy that I have enough legroom on long transcontinental airline flights.

## The Chance to Be a Hero

It's a hallmark of maturity, of growing up and becoming the person you're supposed to be. But as F. Scott Fitzgerald put it, becoming a grown-up is a "terribly hard thing to do. It is much easier to skip it and go from one childhood to another."

Doing a 360 is a painful but liberating process for the manager or aspiring leader. It is in a sense, a personal version of the famous monomyth, or Hero's Journey. Achilles' journey did not end in glory, but yours can.

Joseph Campbell spent decades studying the myths and religions of the world and looking for common themes. Perhaps his most meaningful contribution was his articulation of "the hero with a thousand faces," that figure who kept recurring in great myths and literature around the world.

The monomyth, as Campbell described it, had common themes across cultures, continents and generations: Departure, Initiation and Return. It typically played out thusly:

- A great (or potentially great) person is sent to an otherworldly place or an underworld for an adventure. Often this is a place of exile, resulting from some moral failing or weakness of the hero.
- While in exile, the hero usually receives knowledge from a friend or mentor, which in some cases is a supernatural being. This knowledge is crucial to the hero overcoming great trials and achieving new greatness within.
- Having conquered (with outside help) the new world, the hero returns to their own world, often carrying a boon or blessing for those there. In a sense, the hero has now conquered and improved both worlds.

Consider how prevalent the monomyth is. Do you ever wonder why Pixar films have been so successful? It's not simply due to the outstanding computer animation or the clever characters. They are frequently Campbellian heroic journeys.

In *Ratatouille*, the humble Remy dreams of being a gourmet chef despite the fact that he is, well, a rat. Inspired during a time of trial by a vision of his idol Chef Gasteau, he settles in as an unwelcome but determined cook in the food mecca of Paris. Spoiler alert: At the conclusion Remy is able to offer his cooking talents to rats and humans alike, conquering and bridging both worlds.

In *Cars*, the brash young racecar Lightning McQueen finds himself exiled in off-the-grid Radiator Springs and must perform a series of trials to earn his freedom. Through the aid of the humble people of that town—especially the tutoring of retired racing legend Doc Hudson—he reaches the pinnacle of his profession. In this case, he brings a boon not to his original home but to his adopted home of Radiator Springs.

In *The Incredibles*, a super-powered family lives in literal exile in an era in which superheroes have been forced to retire due to the litigiousness of the general public. The family must come together to fight a dangerous new villain. With the aid of faithful friends, they overcome the villain and are able to embrace openly their identities as heroes. Similar themes run through *Finding Nemo*, *Toy Story* and various other Pixar films.

Of course, think about the father of Pixar: Steve Jobs, whose own life has elements of the Hero's Journey. This was, after all, the genius who made Apple a computer pioneer, but who may have scuttled his own ship in the mid-1980s.

His tendency to constantly war against other Apple executives, notably John Scully, led to his exile. The board informed him he was more trouble than he was worth.

Jobs would eventually return triumphantly to Apple, with his uncompromising thirst for excellence intact—but also with a greater level of self-awareness and enhanced ability to work with others. He would not only go on to make the kind of dent in the universe that he sought to make, he would even spend time toward the end of his life generously sharing wisdom with bitter rivals (which will be discussed in Chapter 3).

If you are a manager of others or a leader of a cause and if you are not satisfied with your station, it is essential to view this part of your journey as the exile. The key, then, to overcoming the exile is a willingness to receive the assistance of other souls who are willing to come to your aid. The wise and practical manager will initiate the process herself, through an intentional 360 process.

**I Cannot Do This Alone**

Consider again the dilemma of the inability of our senses to discern some of the most important aspects of our own identity. We cannot evaluate the very retina that we use to see. We cannot notice what fragrance or aroma proceeds forth from us. If there is a problem, we can rely only on others to help us discover that problem.

In one episode of the gloriously inane yet profound SpongeBob Squarepants, SpongeBob and his starfish friend Patrick watch in horror as they watch others flee from them in a state of fright. They begin to imagine that they are too ugly for the rest of society. At some point, they are able to piece together that they both had consumed onion-peanut sundaes that give them such horrible breath that inevitably chased away anyone around them. Neither one could conclude this for himself; they were both able to sense it for each other.

And who said cartoons aren't deep? Let that be the last bit of encouragement you need to allow others to correct your course as a leader.

## 50  Leadership is Hell

# TWO

## YOUR RADAR WORKS HARDER THAN YOUR COMPASS

**THE ROAD TO HELL:** You walk into a room and immediately start reading other people's feelings. You want everyone to be happy—more importantly, you want them to be happy with *you*—so you're doing a lot, but you feel like you're getting nothing done. You change your mind and your direction in the face of resistance. You've heard that pride is bad; but now you're frustrated because you're neither bold enough to take what you want nor humble enough to settle for less. You have no true north.

**THE ROAD OUT OF HELL:** You remain sensitive to people's feelings, but they do not hold you hostage. You've given yourself permission to initiate—to introduce your own passionately held vision of true north, in order to give people something to stand up for or against. You don't judge your actions solely by how much applause you get: A Simon Cowell can mock your abilities in front of a large audience, but you will not crumble.

## The Two-Headed King

I saw the consummate leader on more than a few occasions. He had two heads, four arms and the perfect combination of a sensitive radar and a strong compass.

That perfect leader was in fact a combination of two persons—Warren Bennis and Steven Sample. Bennis and Sample co-taught an honors class on leadership to USC's best undergraduates for 15 years, during which time it was obvious that they were gaining revelations with each new session.

Bennis had been a distinguished practitioner of leadership, as a former university provost and president. But he made his name as a management guru, studying leadership and advising other practitioners. Sample, on the other hand, was a natural leader who had been a university president for decades (and I'll explain later in this chapter why being president of a major university is one of the toughest leadership challenges imaginable). But Sample was unusually reflective for a natural leader, able to view everyday management through the lenses of history, science and even religion. Pull those two together, and you had Lincoln showing you how it's done.

If you could have fused them into one person, you would have had a damned-near perfect leader. Here's why. It was Bennis who first observed that each of them had something that the other lacked. Bennis had a world-class internal radar. He had a natural and well-honed ability to walk into a room and feel the mood of the various women and men sitting there. He could quickly get a sense of the range of distinct hopes, fears and values that those women and men carried. And he could speak to those hopes, oftentimes losing track of any personal agenda he'd brought into that room.

Sample was the exemplar of a leader with a good internal compass. He had a sense of his own personal true north, and he could stay focused on that, whether earthquakes were rumbling, local riots were raging, or faculty were demanding better parking. Uncertainty didn't seem to be a part of his world. It was magnificent to behold such confidence, even when he met with more powerful people who led more powerful organizations. His assertiveness allowed an academic-looking Midwestern engineer to come across as godlike to most of the people he came into contact with (especially those who worked within his organization).

Sample came to believe that Bennis had developed an ingenious model for leadership. In his bestselling book, *The Contrarian's Guide to Leadership*, he would argue that just a radar or just a compass isn't enough to be a skilled leader.

> The radar-equipped find it hard to stay on course long enough to get anything accomplished, while the gyro-equipped are liable to run into an iceberg at full steam. The contrarian leader knows he should have both.

Serving as I did as Sample's editor at the time, I agreed thoroughly with him. But, I had to ask: "Steve, you've got the compass and Warren has the radar. But if a leader can't have both, which of the two is better to have?"

Sample thought about it, and his response didn't surprise me. "I guess I'd go with my compass," he said, without a trace of arrogance. He explained, and would later write in his book, that if a leader has to choose between being sensitive to others or being able to stay on course, he should choose the latter.

## What's at Stake?

| NATURAL ROLES FOR THOSE WITH STRONG COMPASSES | NATURAL ROLES FOR THOSE WITH STRONG RADARS |
|---|---|
| President | Vice president |
| General | Soldier |
| Dictator | Dictated |
| Lothario | Librarian |
| Party crasher | Party planner |
| White collar criminal | Model citizen |

If you have a strong radar, you have the natural temperament to be a journalist or historian or psychologist or pastor or teacher. But swallow hard: you're probably not a natural leader. If you want to lead other people, you have to work overtime at overcoming your tendency to be pulled by what everyone else feels and wants.

If your radar is much more active than your compass, here are a few problems that commonly result:

- You will lean excessively on the advice of the last person who talked to you.
- You will struggle to fire an underperformer because you care as much about his feelings as you do about the good of the organization that you're trying to lead.
- You will be afraid of taking chances or following your passions.
- Even a modest amount of criticism from others will divert you from your dreams.
- You will be passed over for many management roles, and you will fail to create your own leadership roles.

- If you do get a chance at management by virtue of your intelligence and skills, you will have migraines. This is because you are trying to make every one happy, even though hundreds of thousands of years of human history show that humans don't ever agree.

If you're a Radar Operator, we'll offer you some tips for overcoming that passive tendency and for developing a sense of true north that won't instantly get sabotaged by the first sign of resistance from those around you.

## Six Simple (but Hard) Steps to Charging Up Your Compass

### 1. SURVIVE THE GAME OF "SIMON SAYS"

Do you remember when Taylor Hicks was on top of the world for, oh, about 18 seconds? For some of us that seemed about 18 seconds longer than he deserved to be on top of even a small hill. Hicks won the fifth season of American Idol by doing what he does best, which is ignoring what others think of him. He is the anti-radar. If we can ever put his essence in a bottle, you should buy a case.

Hicks was an unassuming man from Alabama whose hair began to gray at the age of 14. His parents' divorce drove him to blues and soul music, which he took to with awkward relish.

Many Americans of refined taste suffered epileptic seizures when Hicks performed songs such as "Play That Funky Music" by Wild Cherry, while Idol ringleader Simon Cowell often dismissed Hicks' act as bad karaoke by someone who lacked a star's persona. Yet Hicks smiled in the face of such withering criticism, soldiered (with the encouragement of Paula Abdul and Randy Jackson, Idol's less judgmental judges), and eventually won the phone-in vote contest. Cowell admitted he'd been wrong.

Cowell earned respect, contempt and fear as the archetype of the intimidating critic that each person carries in her own mind (and yes, this is typically a projection of a parent, as most any therapist would tell you). We all have hopes, and we all fear that someone who is authoritative, experienced and convincing will scoff at us and attempt to wake us up from silly dreams and make ourselves useful for a change. But Google a video of Hicks' audition for Idol, and you'll see the power of tuning out the Cowells of the world.

Would the criticism of a Simon Cowell freeze you in your tracks? Would it torment you at 3 a.m.? If so, then you're not ready to lead yourself or anyone else in that direction.

If you are a Radar Operator, you must give yourself permission, constantly, to be the measure of all things, instead of taking the measure of all things—to have a conviction that matters at least as much as anyone else's.

## 2. TUNE OUT THE COMMENTS SECTION

You cannot always screen out others' judgments. Nor should you want to. You do need a certain amount of feedback. The danger for the Radar Operator is that she will obsessively seek to know what everyone is saying about her.

When Steve Sample was president of USC, he had an odd habit of not reading news stories about himself. One day I asked him what he thought of a banner headline and story atop the *Los Angeles Times*' sports section, questioning whether he should fire the football coach. Sample asked, in turn, "What did *you* think of it?"

"It seemed to be the usual sensationalism we've come to expect from a lot of media," I said.

Sample said, "Yeah, that's what my lieutenants told me this morning too. But I never read it myself."

"Why not? How could you not read a huge story about yourself, with a color picture of your face splashed across it?"

"I don't need to know," he said, coolly. "I've got a job to do. I don't want to be pulled by the nose by some editor's agenda. If I read it, that editor's agenda will be stuck in my mind. It will influence me more than it needs to. So I just asked my lieutenants if there's anything really important in there that I need to address. They said no, so I moved on."

Not one person in a thousand can resist looking at what a major news institution said about them in such a visible article on the front page. But Sample's reasons were laudable. His compass could be knocked out of commission if he spent his time reading what critics were saying about his actions.

Today managers, public figures, celebrities and politicians are pummeled in the comments sections of online news sites. The smartest ones learn to pay no attention. As an opinion columnist, I won't read them either. The comments section can seem like a holding pen for psychopaths. The anonymous commenters live to blow off steam through the most brutal of condemnations. Ask trusted friends or family members to flag comments of real value and ignore the rest.

### 3. BECOME YOUR OWN *BEST* CRITIC

Like many blowhards, I love to speak. And I love for my speaking to be loved. I mentioned in Chapter 1 how I'd shared with an old mentor, Jim, a metric that I'd concocted to judge how well one of my talks had gone.

I told him, "If someone says, 'That was great, Rob,' then that really means, 'That was pretty good.' If they say, 'That was good,' that really means, 'That was okay.' If they say, 'Thank you for being here today,' that really means, 'Let's agree to move forward and not speak about this incident any further.'"

I do think I was right. What I hadn't mentioned earlier was that Jim was puzzled by my clever observation. "Why do you even need them to tell you whether your talk went well or not?"

"How else could I know whether I did a good job?"

"You can figure that out on your own, Rob." He might as well have been speaking Swahili to me.

I responded, "If I give a talk that the audience thinks was terrible, then it was a terrible talk, right? And if they loved it, then it was a good talk, right?"

"But what if you had to run out of the auditorium to catch a plane as soon as the talk was over? If you couldn't stick around to hear people's comments, couldn't you still judge your talk?"

"No. I don't see how."

"Look, when you got up there to talk, you had a purpose. The purpose wasn't for everyone in the audience to find you attractive. The purpose was to communicate some information, to make a point, to say what needs to be said. You just have to ask yourself, 'Did I say what I needed to be said, as well as I can say it?' And then nothing else matters. You can't control the rest, and you don't need to."

This notion is revelatory for Radar Operators. Every decision he or she makes tends to be done with an eye on generating maximum applause and minimum criticism. Such a person can at best hope to be an entertainer—but not a leader who has someplace to take others.

## 4. NO MORE MR. NICE GUY: FIRE AWAY WITH GRACE

It's been said that public speaking is most people's greatest fear. But really, there is nothing compared to the fear of looking people in the eye and firing them.

In the case of Radar Operators, the idea of firing a person is infinitely harder. They will give second, third and thousandth chances to an underperformer. They will pretend not to notice that things are going poorly. They will pray for an asteroid to strike the earth, in order to spare them from the unpleasantness of it all. What they will not do, as people who live for the feelings (and usually the applause) of others, is make and execute a difficult decision.

The costs are huge. Organizations stagnate when managers are too timid to ease out employees who are underperforming or who are mismatched for the work they've been assigned. Besides, these employees inevitably detect and resent the palpable sense that they're not appreciated. This leads to internal sniping that yanks morale down further and a culture of non-accountability builds. It benefits everyone if the civilized art of "employee liberation" is cultivated.

Many management gurus today speak of creatively finding win-win situations to any controversy. Yet sometimes there are no win-wins, and you must take responsibility for an imperfect outcome.

One effective and principled leader brought up the army ethics test question in which you are told to imagine that you're driving a bus around a narrow mountain curve when you notice a small child walking onto the road. You have enough time to instinctively pull the bus off the road and plunge to your death in order to save the child. Or you have to steel yourself and strike the child because you may have something on board that is even more precious than one child. Remember, there are no win-wins here. You cannot hope to swerve like Speed Racer and avoid the child. You now have to take moral responsibility for a situation that may call for an unpleasant, but inevitable, outcome.

A Radar Operator despises such decisions. But good leadership requires knowing your moral core well enough to deal boldly with complexity. If you're too timid to layoff one underperformer from your struggling business, your whole team (including the star performers) may end up out on the street. Is that right or decent?

I overcame my own Radar Operator tendencies in order to relocate a number of people from jobs that were a poor match for their abilities. It required remembering that I was obligated to the overall good of my organization, not to any one employee. It required becoming clear about how I stated performance expectations and measured that performance. Perhaps above all, it required letting go of the belief that a manager's task is to win the applause and love from colleagues. The poignant irony is that, when done with honesty and integrity, relationships can often endure a firing.

## 5. NO MORE MR. NICE GUY, CONTINUED: FAKE SOME CONFIDENCE

Are you a *nice* man or a *nice* woman? If you are, then we may need to do an intervention before you become a bitter shadow of the person that you could have been.

The would-be leader whose radar is stronger than his or her compass can be likened to the nice guy who complains, "Women prefer jerks." Please forgive any patriarchal or heteronormative undertones here, as I'm sure you can see where we're going with this. See, this nice guy spends his waking hours looking for signs of interest in a woman whom he fancies. He's always looking for clear signs that it's okay for him to pursue a person of interest, without any threat of awkwardness or rejection. He spends his days interpreting data, too nervous to make a move because he senses that he's not getting enough of an opening.

While the nice guy is performing his ritual of hesitations, some ill-bred jerk swoops in and steals the girl away by a remarkable feat of physics. The supposed jerk suggests without hesitation that he finds her intriguing and that he'd like to take her to the flea market this Sunday. She is intrigued and flattered in return. Sparks happen, and potentially a conflagration. The nice guy burns too, watching the scene from a distance, puzzled and angry. His hunch has been confirmed that the universe has been wired for injustice. What he misses is that the woman was not attracted to the jerk's lack of hygiene or moral character; she was attracted to his passion and strength, which represent muscles that the nice guy has refused to develop.

This dynamic works in management and politics as much as in romance. People can smell strength and purpose, as if it were a pheromone, and the primal, reptilian stubs of their brains respond almost magically.

Ronald Reagan may be the modern exemplar. In Reagan's own day, the respect for him was far from universal. The great social critic Neil Postman marveled that, "although our current President, a former Hollywood movie actor, rarely speaks accurately and never precisely, he is known as the Great Communicator." It was because Reagan had a sense of compass that came through, even as he bungled crucial details or made facts up, such as "trees cause more pollution than automobiles do." Say something dumb with sufficient conviction and enough people will let it slide.

"Men tend to believe all that they see is believed in strongly," Nietzsche said.

The first time I'd seen those words was as a caption to a historical photo of an evil demagogue whipping a crowd into a frenzy. The challenge, dear Radar Person, is to convince you that you can be assertive and commanding without becoming an evil demagogue who has to be exiled for the good of the planet.

Most likely, you can pull this off with no such downside. It's been said that you have to bend over backwards just to straighten out your natural curve. So if you tried to be an outright tyrant, you will most likely be just an average person with average assertiveness and that will usually be all that you need! If you merely try to be a person of average assertiveness, you will undercorrect, and people will still be calling you a doormat behind your back.

In the spirit of Nietzsche's words, you also have to immunize yourself somewhat from the certainty with which other people speak. Just because a person seems utterly convinced of his point doesn't mean that he is any more right than you are. Some people are congenitally certain about all things ("sometimes in error, never in doubt," as the saying goes). But resist the temptation to roll over and accept their point of view on faith. Trust your instincts and your ability to contribute to the dialogue.

Great nations, great companies, and great romances are all magnificent forms of collaboration. But they don't just blossom magically, through all sides simultaneously coming to the same conclusion and knowing what to do next. Politics, business, and romance all typically involve one person taking the initiative and a risk. For the Radar Operator, that requires a new way of thinking.

## 6. CHANNEL YOUR INNER TIGER MOM

The typical Radar Operators don't realize it, but they are usually living out the role of the archetypal younger sibling within a family. Their antennas are sensitive to any signals of stress and discord within the family unit, and they feel an anxiety that can't be reduced until they find some way of reducing the anxiety that they see around them. They will bend themselves into whatever shape necessary to please an angry father, a disappointed mother or a demanding older sibling.

It's a nice recipe for a nervous life. But it's the opposite of natural leadership. Small wonder that, by the time they arrive at an office, they have no idea how to play any role other than the people-pleaser.

An effective leader of a group or a nation has many similarities to the mother or father of a family. She acts out of a strong conviction about what would be best for her brood. She asks her friends and relatives for feedback about what school to send her 8-year-old son to, but she leaves the decision to herself, not to a poll. She cares deeply about her son's feelings but doesn't quickly back down on a decision simply because he feels strongly otherwise. Her compass works just fine, thank you.

The irony is that parents today, especially in the United States, may be more lenient and less authoritative than at any time in history. When news media run stories about "tiger moms" who push their children to excel, many people react with alarm. Yet for our purposes, the Radar Operator can benefit by tapping into the alpha authority of such a parent who rigidly shapes her family's future.

## 7. MANAGE YOUR ENERGY, NOT YOUR WORDS

Many civilized people are more hesitant than they need to be. When they speak up, they tend to worry about exactly which words to use. That only makes them more hesitant, and thus less effective, less commanding and less convincing as leaders.

It's not what you say, it's how you say it. When you have to give a speech or make a pitch, your words don't matter as much as your energy. "Energy" may be a bit of a new-agey, touchy-feely, 21$^{st}$ century word. Whereas a traditional person might say, "Jillian has a warm spirit," someone today would exclaim, "Jillian's got a really good energy." The point is that energy is that thing that radiates from you—and when a good energy is radiating from you, your words quite naturally tend to be effective. When you seem to be sitting in a puddle of weak or timid energy, even the most brilliant words won't have much effect.

We know this because human beings have been an evolutionary work in progress for millions of years—yet language has been around for only a small portion of that time. So for the greatest part of human history, we evolved to read one another's posture, attitude, facial and vocal cues.

These interaction references haven't changed. A study from UCLA several years ago estimated that, when you speak, an audience's impression of you is based 55 percent on how you come across visually. About 38 percent of that impression involves how you sound, while the remaining seven percent involves the precise words you say. It sounds astounding and impossible—but you know it's true when you realize how so many celebrities and politicians make quite a living despite lacking verbal skills or common sense!

The quick upshot is this: When preparing to present yourself, at some point beforehand you should stop trying to think about what to say and start getting into the right frame of mind. Relax, take deep breaths and maybe even watch a funny YouTube video. Then practice the art of cultivating your strongest and most commanding presence.

## Reality Check for the Radar Operator: Why Do I Want to Lead?

Many people with excellent radars think that it would be wonderful to be in charge. After all, they may be more intelligent, more sensitive, more fragrant and more decent than the ogres and alpha-figures who usually end up in charge. But just because you're awesome doesn't mean you're ready to be a manager or a leader.

Do yourself a favor and reflect honestly on whether you'd be happiest as a leader in your field, in your community, in your church or temple, in your local PTA or even in your own family. This is a recurring theme within these chapters. You may be someone who would thrive more in a myriad of other roles, free of the headaches that only leaders and managers know.

In the end, you have to be honest with yourself: Do I actually have someplace that I want to take people? Or do I just like the idea of people following me around? If it's the latter (and all too often, if you're honest, it is), you'll be miserable and so will the people who are wondering why on earth they're following you around while you're walking in circles.

David Gergen, author of *Eyewitness to Power*, observed that having a real place to take people is what separated many successful presidents from those who stumbled or brought embarrassment on themselves and others. Ronald Reagan, as Gergen notes, had a clear vision for what he wanted to happen, namely reduced tax burdens and a strong military.

## CASE STUDIES IN RADARITIS

### All Dressed Up with Nowhere to Lead

George H.W. Bush was destined to be president for a reason: It would look fantastic on his resume. (We're not saying it was a good reason.) Bush Senior would not go down in history as a successful president, in most senses of the word, even though he was an eminently decent man. It's quite possible that he will go down in history as that guy who couldn't even get re-elected against a candidate who was dismissed as a womanizing draft-dodger.

Bush, who served with distinction as one of America's youngest naval aviators on the Pacific front during World War II, was a man with an excellent radar and little compass. He succeeded Ronald Reagan, who was almost entirely compass in constitution. That change seemed refreshing for a while, as Bush spoke of nurturing a "kinder, gentler" society.

Many of Bush's most important jobs were appointed positions. As a good follower who had the good sense to send an endless flood of warm, hand-written notes to colleagues and bosses, he ended up as the United States' ambassador to the United Nations, an envoy to China, chairman of the Republican National Committee, and director of the Central Intelligence Agency. By contrast, whenever he ran for elected office, he usually lost. But as the son of Senator Prescott Bush, he believed he was destined for great things.

Because he was fundamentally a good man with solid principles, he achieved some success on his watch, notably in the area of foreign relations. He could be seen as a decent manager of American interests. Yet when the economy slowed, Bush was seen as vacillating and ineffective. After making himself famous for refusing to raise taxes, he agreed to raise taxes; this may have been good policy, but it was bad politics, as it exposed his compass as a flimsy one.

Jonathan Alter, in critiquing Bush late in his first term, offered one of the most meaningful definitions of leadership: "Anyone can take people where they already want to go," Alter wrote. "True leaders can take people where only better selves dare to tread. That's where the leader's values come in. They must want to do something with their power—not just be powerful."

Bush Sr. believed he in some way deserved to be president of the United States, but did not actually have a compelling direction in which to take its citizens. That led to an unceremonious exit from a White House he seemingly spent all his life trying to reach.

Bill Clinton would replace Bush and, despite being one of this generation's shrewdest political operators, would struggle to find his footing for a few years. Many critics have argued that Clinton lacked the sort of compass and character that Reagan had. And he seemed to be confused at times about whether to be a liberal president or a centrist one. But Clinton deserves some credit for reinventing himself, after the Republican sweep in the 1994 midterm elections, as an effective, post-ideological steward of his nation's economy and foreign policy.

That remains Clinton's brand. For a man who once kept his eye too closely on his popularity ratings, he is now more popular than ever—a gaudy 69 percent favorability rating, even in our toxically partisan political environment.

**Dreaming Worthy Dreams**

Having spent endless hours chairing committees and groups within a historic Presbyterian church, I often found myself leading the church's large group of young adults. Nominating committees would elect members of my leadership team, some of whom were gifted and some of whom were malcontents. These nominating committees believed that, if someone complained about how the group functioned, becoming a part of the leadership team would be a fantastic way for them to constructively engage and grow.

Kelly was one such person. She longed to be valued, she longed to participate, and she longed to be a part of something big. Yet she had no true north. She did have management "wisdom" on her side. She would take me to coffee and show me management books with flow charts and diagrams that stated with grim authority that effective organizations resulted from groups that collaborated in discerning a vision.

But Kelly lived in something of a dream world, a fantasy realm inhabited by many experts on leadership who believe in touchy-feely ideals. Rather, Kelly wanted everyone in our leadership committee to spend endless hours "discerning together" what true north looked like for our organization. The other committee members had no such enthusiasms. Kelly proposed weekend-long retreats to discuss vision, and the others discussed having her removed from the committee.

She dreamed of having everyone discover a common dream. She felt miserable about not being able to get everyone to discover a common dream. Ultimately she became their harshest critic because she blamed them for ruining her own deep hopes. What Kelly actually needed to do was to give herself permission to dream her own dream, to articulate her dream to others and then to negotiate her dream in order to engage them into it.

It's for this reason that I wince when anyone in an organization whips out a white board and dry-erase marker and says, "Okay, let's discuss all the goals we all have here." The person may get a conversation going, but generally won't achieve any change within the organization. In trying to be a facilitator, he or she won't be a leader.

## Mission Statement Madness

Daniel was a successful CFO of a corporation, and he had a problem similar to Kelly's. Daniel felt held back. He sensed that those who tended to get the CEO jobs were less visionary, less shrewd and less intelligent than him. He knew he could outperform his boss if he only got the chance.

He was invited to join the board of a charity that served low-income families. Given his credentials, other board members began pushing him to take his leadership skills out for a spin as the board chairman for this organization, which was continually wrestling with how to slice a meager annual budget closer to the bone.

Daniel demurred on the chair position a year or two, which frustrated other board members. At the same time, Daniel had been pushing them to create a new mission statement.

Some board members told Daniel that the current mission statement, something vague about helping those in need nearby, seemed adequate for the task. He argued it was too broad and too vague and too, well, boring.

"A good mission statement has to be compelling," he said. "It needs to crystalize what you're about and why you're needed. Once you do that, the wallets fly open, and you'll get all the money you need."

That seemed compelling, and they established a new mission statement committee, with Daniel at the helm. The new mission statement was slapped onto posters and postcards and newsletters and emails, but wallets did not fly open, either immediately or after Daniel finally accepted the chairmanship of the charity.

Daniel did manage to put his CFO skills to use, as he worked with others to hand off the organization to a larger national organization. But why didn't his efforts to lead have the consequences he expected? Why did the organization not come together with a clear sense of purpose? Why did the wallets refuse to fly open? Why did the vision of this bright and successful money man not come to life? Two reasons stand out.

As was the case with Matthew in Chapter 1, Daniel's radar led him to believe that, by giving others a space in which to share their hopes and dreams, any consensus that they reach will have supernatural consequences. That idealism generally fails the real-world test. After endless bickering and negotiating and compromising, the new mission statement looked remarkably similar to the original. Potential donors were unmoved to give, and current donors were unmoved to give more.

Second, it became evident that, while Daniel was a skilled manager, he wasn't meant to be the leader of a charity such as this one. He lacked a true north as it related to the group. The group's mission wasn't of deep personal interest to him. He chose to give his money generously—but to *other* organizations. He was willing nevertheless to accept the challenge of guiding this group through the muck, but with some failed assumptions. Daniel expected the others to discern a new direction and articulate a new vision that everyone could feel passionate about, but he himself wasn't passionate enough to pull them together. In other words, he was willing to be *in charge*, but he wasn't willing to *lead*.

Would-be leaders often feel that *their* leaders haven't been listening to them. They decide that, if they're in charge, they will be master listeners. But if you only listen, and you aren't driven by your own sense of true north, you may hear crickets, or you may hear a confusing and conflicting cacophony of sounds.

The mission statement experience that USC President Steve Sample (one of the ultimate Compass Operators) had was almost the reverse. Sample was clear about true north for his organization. A trustee of the university, who was a legendary business leader, suggested to Sample that he should be able to summarize that sense of true north in a mission statement, "no longer than one page, in 12-point type."

That may seem rather long but bear in mind that we're talking about academia here. Sample personally drafted a page describing USC's key roles, priorities and mission; and then he sent the document out widely for discussion and revision. Unlike Daniel, Sample led the process aggressively. In the end, he had a mission statement with broad consent, one that he could quote as Scripture-like rationale for his decisions and actions.

One could easily make the case that Sample didn't create a truly collaborative, organic process for discerning a collective vision. One could make the case that the right method lies somewhere between Sample's approach and Daniel's approach.

But in the spirit of what Sample told me, cited earlier in this chapter, if you can't have a perfect balance of radar and compass, it's better to err on the side of the compass.

## Success Story: From Radar to a Balanced Radar-Compass

In our business-obsessed society, being the president or chancellor of a major university isn't as glamorous a leadership position as being the CEO of a publicly traded company.

But it's much harder.

How could that be? I've watched and worked with both kinds of leaders up close.

The tenured faculty is considered the foundation of a university; that means people who cannot be fired or reassigned are your major constituency. Running a university isn't even possible, because the de facto CEO can't fire or even reassign many of the most opinionated and noisiest constituencies.

She can rarely fall back on pure exercises of authority that the ordinary CEO thrives on. She must work with critics, using powers of persuasion to talk dogs off meat trucks and get different internal fiefdoms to cooperate.

She also typically deals with students, angry parents, politicians, funding agencies and tens of thousands of alumni who have their own agendas and whose donations are essential to the institution's survival. If running a vast academic enterprise isn't enough, she has to deal with the related enterprises — a vast housing and dining complex, a private police force and a few major athletic franchises.

Small wonder that Herman Wells, the former president of the Indiana University, speculated that the ideal university president would combine "the physical charm of a Greek athlete, the cunning of Machiavelli, the wisdom of Solomon, the courage of a lion, the skin of a rhino and the stomach of a goat."

Because that role may be the most challenging management role possible, leadership expert Warren

Bennis sensed several decades ago that he needed to move from theory to practice, which soon led him to serve as the president of the University of Cincinnati. There he took his family, his world-renowned organizational management theories and his finely tuned radar.

He was still at the office at 4 o'clock one morning, almost a year into his presidency, when he received an internal wakeup call.

He had been spending the pre-dawn hours sifting through stacks of memos and letters that shouted at him for his attention and assistance. He was overwhelmed, and he realized he risked doing much while getting nothing done.

For a Radar Operator such as Bennis, it would have seemed impossible to ignore the stack of mail. Angry letters came from alumni and locals about a range of issues. In one case, a progressive education dean had begun bringing his baby to the office some days, to share in parenting duties and allow his wife to continue her own career. Soon the situation drew national media attention from critics who on one side accused the dean of child abuse and who on the other side accused him of not taking his work duties seriously. The university's hospital was also mired in a messy national controversy regarding human tests involving radiation.

This was not an issue of efficiency. The existence of email at the time would not have sped up his response time. Bennis at last determined he would accomplish nothing of lasting significance if he only attended to the concerns of others. But his solution wasn't to go to bed, get some sleep and wake up intent on ignoring others' concerns. Rather, he decided to assemble a more appropriate team of lieutenants surrounding him, and to trust them to deal with many of the concerns and action steps—so that Bennis could continue the business of leading the organization where he believed it needed to go. Less radar for Bennis, and much more compass.

How would he build such a team, which he grandly called an "executive constellation"? He decided upon two factors: 1) Each lieutenant had to know more about his or her area than the president knew; and 2) each lieutenant had to be ready and able to take appropriate action within his or her area without checking back with the president for guidance or handholding.

That freed Bennis up to focus more on the larger picture. (In the next chapter, we'll see that no leader can focus only on the big picture, but in this case Bennis was finally able to get to the greater issues.)

Controversies subsided, but the most pressing issue was the financial viability of the university itself. This private university was a symbol of civic pride for Cincinnatians, but it needed millions of dollars more annually than it was able to bring in. That money, however, wasn't going to be found within city limits or county limits. Bennis arrived at the conclusion that, if the university were to survive, it would need to go public, affiliating with the state of Ohio. Yet the notion repelled the fiercely independent citizens of the Cincinnati community. They could not risk their beloved University of Cincinnati to become just another campus of the Ohio State University system.

What would a classic Radar Operator do in such a situation? He or she would gauge their followers' interest, sense that it's lacking, give up on the plan, hope a new and easier one comes along, test that idea out, sense that it's lacking, rinse and repeat.

Instead Bennis locked in on his true north. He built a campaign machine of sorts, who would help persuade various constituencies inside the university and the city, and around the state.

His radar did not disappear—rather it worked in perfect tandem with his compass. This allowed his team to understand and then speak to various hopes and anxieties among the constituencies. They were able to convince their academic community and the local community that the university would maintain its status and role as an anchor for the city, while reducing local taxes. They simultaneously worked on persuading state legislators that, for Ohio to succeed, it needed a strong and thriving institution in Cincinnati. What began as a longshot ended with 70 percent of Cincinnati voters approving a referendum on state affiliation. A leading state legislator even called to beg Bennis to "call off the dogs," after being so impressed and overwhelmed by the lobby effort.

Bennis' university went on to thrive, because a man noted mainly for his radar became an exemplar of a leader with a perfect *blend* of radar and compass.

This is not to say that Bennis felt he needed to spend the remainder of his career playing such roles. Cincinnati is named for Cincinnatus, the Roman statesman who gave up ultimate authority to return to private life and who stands as the counterpoint to the leader who clings to power. Bennis would ironically be something of a Cincinnatus for Cincinnati. Not long afterward, he realized he loved the life of the curious scholar, and that he felt passionate about studying leadership in a way that allowed him to guide and coach other leaders. Yet now he could guide them having successfully inhabited the breach between radar and compass.

# THREE

## YOUR COMPASS WORKS HARDER THAN YOUR RADAR

**THE ROAD TO HELL:** You're trampling people on your way to your goals. You're aware that other people have their own feelings and agendas, but you're not entirely sure what that has to do with getting yourself and others moving toward your true north. You have certainty about your direction, just like all those other people who raced off cliffs while trying to reach the stars.

**THE ROAD OUT OF HELL:** You move toward your true north with an infectious energy—but you also can adjust course before you race off a cliff. You're convincing, but you're not pig-headed. You can walk into the room and take the crowd's temperature, getting a sense for the hopes and goals of those around you. People truly follow you—they don't simply get dragged around by you anymore.

## Know What You Do

Do you have an overactive compass and an underactive radar? Ask yourself if one of these two statements applies strongly in your life:

1. I'm frustrated. I've been trying to get others to understand where we need to go in order to move our organization forward, but they stubbornly resist. They argue back.
2. I'm fine. My employees don't argue with me as much as they used to. Now they carry out what I tell them to do.

It turns out that either of these two scenarios may show that your compass is too active. In either scenario, you may be trying to treat employees like pawns to be moved around the chessboard, without benefiting from the feedback they can give you from their unique vantage points. Profiting from feedback can serve your career; ignoring it can ruin it.

If Scenario 1 applies to you, you may be spinning your wheels in vain, while frustrating those around and under you. If Scenario 2 applies to you, you may be making great progress in getting everyone to charge forward . . . off a cliff.

If Scenario 1 applies to you, you may not need to blame yourself entirely—even the Lord was said to be sick and tired of the "stiff-necked" people he was trying to guide out of Egypt and through the desert to the Promised Land. On a couple of occasions, the Lord urged Moses to get rid of his current flock of followers and find a more cooperative bunch.

As managers, many times changing your followers is not an option. Hence there is a sweet spot to locate— an ideal balance of healthy inner confidence and healthy respect for the views of others.

If you've been told by your mother or sibling or friends that you're quite a strong-willed person, you need to consider strongly that you're hardheaded to a fault. Loved ones who make such an observation about you may see it as an asset, but they're surely being more charitable than others who can derail your career.

You need to go back to Chapter 1 and assess whether you have a blind spot. Ask yourself, too, how often you change your mind when others give you new information or when others ask you to reconsider your position. Do you take pride in being resolute?

That pride may ruin you.

## A Certain Amount of Certainty Is *Good*

If you watched the 2012 U.S. presidential debates, you know that some of the world's smartest (or at least, best-paid) pundits spent hours analyzing which presidential or vice presidential candidate seemed more confident and emphatic about whatever exaggerations, distortions or untruths he uttered. Sure, there were the surreyed ranks of "fact checkers" who weighed in, but their job was mostly to remind everyone that all candidates exaggerate. The real action, though, was in praising whichever side exaggerated with greater élan and a greater sense of impunity.

It's a reminder that Neil Postman was right three decades ago when he wrote books such as *Amusing Ourselves to Death: Public Discourse in the Age of Show Business*. Postman argued that television had made a society dependent on image and theater rather than facts and reason. The age of Twitter made his truths look doubly true.

Go back to Nietzsche's observation that people tend to believe all that they see is believed in strongly. It explains why hucksters are able to sell us real estate in

Kandahar even when we brace ourselves against their persuasions. It explains why we elect and re-elect lying politicians while shrugging and fuming that "they all do that."

## A Certain Other Amount of Certainty is *Bad*

Yes, there *is* a case for avoiding certainty.

"The fruitfulness of our lives depends in large measure on our ability to doubt our own words and to question the value of our own work," the legendary monk Thomas Merton observed more than a half-century ago. "The man who completely trusts his own estimate of himself is doomed to sterility."

If you are a person with a strong compass, you naturally find it hard to doubt your own words or to question the value of your own work. The hardest chore on your list is "doubting" your own estimate of yourself.

But it's crucial. Psychologists have thoroughly documented how most people tend to think they're smarter and funnier and more competent and more empathetic than they really are. Studies routinely show that six out of 10 people believe they have above average intelligence—or that seven in 10 people believe that people are selfish, while only a small percentage admit that they themselves are selfish. Someone is wrong here.

Here's the rub: The person who is filled with doubt builds little of enduring value. But the person who has no capacity to doubt may build aggressively but bring the whole enterprise down in an unscheduled blaze.

Where is the sweet spot, where is that Goldilocks zone, with the "just right" blend of confidence and doubt? Where is that psychic, intellectual and emotional space where a person's convictions are firm but not rigid?

## Unlike Father, Unlike Son

George W. Bush wasn't fated by the stars to be a controversial and unpopular president.

Whereas his father, George H.W. Bush was a Radar-Driven Manager who lacked an intuitive sense of true north, W. became the poster child for the Compass-Driven Manager who lacked a sensitive radar, and he paid a steep price for it.

The typical criticisms and defenses of Bush, who left office with a 34 percent approval rating amidst two costly wars and an economic meltdown, miss the point. It wasn't that he lacked sufficient intelligence or that he was a victim of dark fortune beyond his control.

Bush was able to defeat the radar-driven Al Gore in 2000, within a campaign where economic tranquility should have given Gore's incumbent Democrats an insurmountable edge. Yet Bush's authenticity, his self-confidence and his certainty looked more attractive over a long campaign than Gore's nervous, weather-vane, please-like-me approach. Later, it was Bush's resolution that allowed him to achieve an approval rating near 90 percent among his citizens after the shock of 9/11. Few persons in America doubted, in the months afterward, that Bush didn't have the potential to be a Rushmorean president because of his strong compass.

But it was Bush's compass and his sense of moral certainty that drove him off the cliff of Iraq and subsequent political calamities.

That gave an opening to his challenger, John Kerry, in 2004. Despite the rising unpopularity of Bush, Kerry trailed in the polls. Like Gore, Kerry was a radar-driven manager, which meant that he lacked the confidence pheromone that attracts voters away from a politically damaged compass-driven manager.

Yet Kerry scored heavy political points in a debate with Bush in October 2004, by framing Bush's greatest strength as a liability.

"It's one thing to be certain," he told Bush. "But you can be certain and be wrong. Certainty sometimes can get you in trouble."

Kerry put into words what Americans had been feeling during that long slide from euphoria. From that point forward, the race tightened. Bush gained a narrow victory. Rather than being chastened and seeking to pay more attention to other viewpoints, he declared after the election, "I earned political capital and I intend to spend it."

After bankrupting himself of such capital in a short time, one of history's ironies is that Bush seemed to develop a better radar. He began taking seriously the cautions of his more radar-driven lieutenants, such as Condoleeza Rice. He replaced the reckless Donald Rumsfeld with Robert Gates, a bipartisan operative with world-class radar and principles. Vice President Dick Cheney, immune to political empathy, grew increasingly sidelined.

Bush had already been too bruised by the crashing about of his first term to recover fully. When the economic meltdown occurred, the negative aspects of his legacy were frozen in the public's mind.

Yet if the measured Bush of 2007 had been in operation in 2003, history (or at least his legacy) could have been quite different. The further irony is that this more radar-driven Bush had been on display before, as a fairly effective governor of Texas.

The best guess would be that some combination of pride, a fear of inadequacy in being in the White House at such a momentous time, and the egging on of Cheney and Rumsfeld fired up Bush's own natural compass, while shutting down his radar altogether for several years. The results are something for all of us to rue.

## The Jobs Conundrum

The late Apple founder and icon Steve Jobs presents a challenge for aspiring leaders. There are reasons to emulate him and reasons not to. The most obvious reason to imitate him is that he was spectacularly successful. The most obvious reason not to imitate him is that he believed in "thinking different" and blazing one's own trail—so to imitate him would be self-defeating. Not everyone is motivated in the same way and to the same degree that Jobs was motivated. Not everyone is as brilliant and not everyone is as lucky as Steve Jobs was.

Even his extraordinary run of good fortune ended from time to time, notably when Apple's board jettisoned him in 1985 after he'd broken more management china than they felt they could clean up. To a great extent, he only would go on to become the Steve Jobs of legend because his rougher sides were melted and refined in the searing heat of life's crucible, after his difficulties during his first stint at Apple.

A year after Jobs' death, one of his most brilliant protégés, Scott Forstall (who developed Apple's mobile operating system), would be pushed out. The cause was reportedly Forstall's inability to play nice in the sandbox and his refusal to listen to the other brilliant minds at the Cupertino empire. Others depicted him as polarizing and divisive, a know-it-all who couldn't learn from others. Tech bloggers reported that he was a roadblock to collaboration within a company in which others prized collaboration. In other words, he was all compass and no radar.

Forstall was also described by insiders as a "hard-working genius," a "mini-Steve Jobs" and potentially an eventual CEO for Apple. His crashed tenure illustrates an important truth: Being *like* Steve Jobs is not sufficient for achieving a career or legacy like that of Steve Jobs. For a while, Forstall was able to succeed, because Jobs was willing to protect him even as Forstall alienated indispensable figures like legendary design guru Jony Ive. Other executives eventually reportedly grew tired of playing babysitter, Forstall became dispensable and a bright 15-year career at Apple was derailed. If Forstall is as lucky as Steve Jobs, he may come back someday triumphantly—but not without having paid life's heavy toll in building a radar from scratch.

### Tuning in to Your Advisers' Frequencies

Let's concede that a manager with a strong compass and weak radar has two advantages over the manager with the strong radar and weak compass. First, as noted in the previous chapter, people with strong compasses more naturally fall into leadership roles. Second, a leader with a weak radar can offset some of her liabilities by surrounding herself with advisers who have strong radars. By contrast, a manager who has a weak compass needs to develop an adequate one of her own; she can't delegate that out to a lieutenant or to a committee.

A team of lieutenants with strong radars can serve as a field of human weathervanes for the Compass-Driven Manager, helping him to recognize undercurrents and crosscurrents that could endanger the enterprise.

### Better a Team of Rivals than a Team of Parrots

Abraham Lincoln brought together a rowdy collection of voices in his cabinet, as Doris Kearns Goodwin illustrated in *Team of Rivals: The Political Genius of Abraham Lincoln*, (which inspired the Steven

Spielberg movie). It takes a person of rare character to stock a cabinet of advisers with former party rivals the way Lincoln did. These brilliant men could not get along well with one another or with Lincoln, but Lincoln decided that he and the country needed their contributions.

Lincoln allowed them to be candid and to bicker openly, during one of the most delicate and labile moments in American history. Because Lincoln had a strong compass, he knew when he needed to heed the advice of his rivals and when he needed to ignore it. He chose to take deep breaths and overlook petty slights, jealousies and bickering.

In time, men such as William Seward, his Secretary of State and the onetime favorite for the 1860 Republican Party nomination, would go on to praise Lincoln as the finest human being he had ever known. Seward, a onetime nemesis, would spend hours huddled with Lincoln, sharing stories and anecdotes.

Former USC President Steve Sample had an almost preternatural sense of confidence. He exuded confidence and certainty, never looking intimidated by any person or circumstance. Occasionally, his confidence could cause him to miss signals of opposition from others. He came to depend deeply on his vice president for public relations, Martha Harris, who had an outstanding radar, along with complete alignment with Sample's goals for his organization. Over time, Sample found he could continue to trust his own instincts, but he gave Harris special permission to throw up red flags. He knew Harris cared deeply about the organization *and* about him, and would step in and speak up whenever the two interests diverged.

## "None of Us Is as Smart as All of Us": The Practical Case for a Radar

You may not have a point of view about the theological concept of original sin, or you may disagree strongly with that concept. But there is a near-universal view, among enduring worldwide philosophies and religions, that pride is the primal imperfection that taints most of human existence. Yet it's more complicated than that. Pride seems to be a building block of individual and collective human identity, while also seeming to be a curse.

Pride—or an active ego—makes and breaks leaders. It is the force that motivates a leader to take risks, to throw a nation on her back and carry it forward, and to make a difference where others have given up hope. It is also the force that makes the leader tune out all counsel from others and allows her to believe that she can be the hero all by herself.

To make the greatest difference, and at least to minimize the chance of running off a cliff, the Compass Jockey has to develop an appreciation for the collective wisdom of others. To put it another way, it means that a person has to fall in love with the concept of democracy; not just with the sentimental, flag-waving tributes, but with a deep understanding of why a democratic approach to governance beats a "pipe down and follow me because I know where we should be going" approach.

The Compass-Driven Leader, convinced of his rightness, often naturally sees the world in Lone Hero terms. If you're such a person, no one is going to "reach" you by grabbing you by the lapels, shaking you, and shouting, "Get over yourself!" Instead, we need you to realize that you can best reach your destination by allowing others to take more responsibility for the journey—for the direction you take together, for the speed at which you move, and for the course adjustments along the way.

**Pericles vs. Plato**

Pericles, that towering figure of a golden age in Athens, offered his legendary funeral oration early in the Peloponnesian War to pay tribute to warriors who fell in the cause of defending their nascent experiment in democracy.

Pericles, like Lincoln two-plus millennia later, noted that the stakes were cosmic in nature. Democratic Athens (okay, it was only democratic if you were a free, land-owning adult male, but it was still a start) was under attack by Sparta and its nondemocratic allies. Government of, by and for the people was a young concept, but Pericles believed it would endure and eventually be imitated by all other governments. Today, *democracy* has good connotations and *tyrant* has negative ones; but it was the other way around before the Athenian experiment.

Democracy had nonetheless been mocked by Athens' invaders as effete—all talk and no action. Pericles instead argued in his funeral oratory that democracy was the only path for truly bold action, because it would only take action that resulted from the, well, "deliberate deliberation" of myriad viewpoints, perspectives and experiences. Democratic action had broader and deeper buy-in than actions taken by nations ruled by one man and his single internal compass.

A generation later Athenians were able to begin reestablishing democracy. It was around this time that Socrates articulated a certain contempt for popular rule—which was most likely the real cause of his death sentence, as historian I. F. Stone has argued. His cynicism rattled Athenians during that fragile moment when they were attempting to reassert democracy.

Plato, falling not far from Socrates' tree, believed that "until wise philosophers are kings, or the kings and princes of this world have the spirit and power of philosophy, and political greatness and wisdom meet in one, and those commoner natures who pursue either to the exclusion of the other are compelled to stand aside, cities will never have rest from their evils."

Obviously Plato was a certain kind of a compass man. He didn't believe that a leader needed to build a good radar. He simply believed that a leader needed to build the best possible compass.

Plato was wrong. We can say that not just from the viewpoint of what C.S. Lewis called "chronological snobbery," in which we claim that anything we do today must inherently be better than what our forebears did. We can say it from what we've learned about human organizations.

### The Real Wisdom of the Mob

James M. Surowiecki, in *The Wisdom of Crowds: Why the Many Are Smarter Than the Few and How Collective Wisdom Shapes Business, Economies, Societies and Nations*, articulated a startling reality: The mob usually knows better than the experts.

That deserves some explanation. This isn't praise for groupthink, which is deadly, when either a large mob or a small group of experts partakes of it. Rather, take the old carnival game of guessing how many jellybeans are in a jar. If you had a choice between relying on the best estimate of an expert on jellybeans or on taking the *average* answer of the larger, uneducated mob, take the uneducated mob every time. Their answer, averaged out, is often dead-on accurate. That's because each member of the mob brings some distinct perspective or insight or knowledge. And aggregating that perspective often gives us the best possible view of reality.

In other words, a strong leader who thinks she knows her way around has a lot to learn from people far lower down the ladder. You see a similar group-wisdom dynamic on trivia game shows, when the average audience answer to a tricky question ends up being right more often than the answer from your brainy Uncle Andrew. (And if you ever get on "The Price Is Right," pay attention to the crowd when it's telling you to bid "higher, higher!")

So Plato, that advocate for philosopher-kings and disrespecter of popular opinion, was wrong: None of us is as smart as all of us. Pericles was right: The boldest citizenry is the one that takes action based on its collective wisdom.

Yet the faith that we place in one powerful, godlike leader (or one small and powerful elite) is a resilient one within human history. Democracy would disappear for centuries until the right set of conditions resurrected it in the young United States.

Even still, most organizations ran in hierarchical ways. The democratic theory of modern management arose only a little over a half-century ago, to some extent as a result of social science research conducted by Warren Bennis and his colleagues. After the horrors of World War II, they searched for how to grow healthy organizations and healthy societies.

Bennis, for his part, conducted experiments that confirmed that, for simple tasks under static conditions, an autocratic, centralized structure is the most efficient. But for complex tasks under changing conditions, a decentralized and democratic model worked better. Whenever complexity was involved, it helped to have a free and open exchange of multiple viewpoints. The greatest reality of our time is an escalation of change and complexity—and the upshot is that democratic approaches are more important than ever in navigating complex and changing landscapes.

Ancient Athens made regular use of a *kleroterion*, a randomly selected group of citizens picked daily to gather, discuss issues and make decisions for the larger city. Stanford professor James Fishkin found that this approach to "deliberative democracy" works just as well today, in our more complex environment. "If people think their voice actually matters, they'll do the hard work, really study their briefing books, ask the experts smart questions and then make tough decisions," he told TIME magazine. "When they hear the experts disagreeing, they're forced to think for themselves. About 70 percent change their minds in the process." He guided such processes in locations around the world and found that deliberative democracy consistently resulted in better outcomes than a smart elite could have dictated.

**Cockpit Resource Management**

Around the world, rigid hierarchical chains of command were being toppled because they courted disaster. A co-pilot in many cases wasn't supposed to second-guess a pilot but when this led to crashes, it was simple common sense—as opposed to nice manners or sentimentality—that made airlines give a green light to a more casual and less hierarchical exchange of information.

Similar approaches took hold in medicine and space aeronautics. When lives were at stake, tolerance shrank for the concept that the bold leader's sense of true north should never be questioned. His or her peers had permission—nay, a duty—to butt in when necessary to redirect a situation to a safer conclusion.

There are more poetic reasons for the Compass-Driven Leader to let others get involved in steering the enterprise. Many of humanity's most momentous innovations resulted from collaboration, not individual genius. What one person invented the Internet? What one person invented the computer? What one person developed the atomic bomb for the Allies before Hitler's Germany could develop one? The Manhattan Project was an example of collaborative genius that couldn't have resulted from individual geniuses working in separate spaces with separate missions.

In developing an effective radar, the Compass-Driven Manager needs to learn an appreciation for when to compromise. At times she will need to craft creative compromise positions among multiple agendas of constituencies. Sometimes she will need to just back down from her own strongly held position, at least temporarily.

You can certainly decide to listen to your employees' advice but not heed it. But if you do so on a regular basis, know that they may decide to play it safe for the sake of their own careers and stop giving you their honest opinion. This lack of candor wouldn't serve you or your organization and it may get all of you in trouble—but it would be almost entirely your fault.

In developing a radar, the Compass-Driven Manager also needs to learn an appreciation for when not to compromise. In some cases, this means abandoning her own opinion, or even the general consensus of her advisers, to pick out one person's brilliant idea and raise it above all others. In that sense, the leader must serve like a prospector, sifting carefully for flecks of gold.

This can be liberating for the strong-willed leader. You don't always have to be the smartest person in the room, you just have to give permission for the smartest idea to rise up and win the day.

Have you ever wondered why so many corporate or political entities seem to offer ordinary, vanilla products and ideas? It's not necessarily because they're afraid and it's certainly not because they're dumb. It's because their decisions are often a bloodless hybrid of many people's ideas.

You sit and wonder: why doesn't any company (or politician) come out and do the obvious thing by striking out in a new and bold direction? The answer is usually that there's someone in every organization championing such a bold direction. But there are plenty of others who say that'd be certain suicide, or who say, "Yes, but let's add on this odd feature." What results is a chimera that's quite unattractive.

Companies like Sony suffered from weak-sauce agreements to disagree on what sorts of new music players could replace their famed Walkman. Meanwhile, Apple boldly shifted to its digital iPod, and corporate history was etch-a-sketched. Apple became the biggest player in music and Sony became a marginal opponent. Now you may be tempted to think that this was a victory for Steve Jobs' compass style over Sony's democratic style. The difference, however, is that Jobs knew when to let Jony Ive or others win the day.

**Success Story: Google's Algorithm Machine Gets Tough Human Feedback from a Tough Human**

Some who have dealt with Google co-founder Larry Page have claimed that he is overly headstrong, with a "smarter than thou" attitude. Google's original marketing chief Douglas Edwards suggested that Page embodied a "math good, humans bad" form of intellectual snobbery at a company legendary for its high intellectual standards.

The strong-willed nature of Page and his peers did cause a rift between onetime collaborators Google and Apple. Steve Jobs, who had taken Page and his partner Sergey Brin under his wing, was enraged when Google began developing Android as a competitor to his iPhone. Jobs famously vowed to wage "thermonuclear war" against Google not long before he died.

To Page's credit, once he had replaced Eric Schmidt as CEO in 2011, he had the humility to reach out sincerely for Jobs' counsel on how to be a good CEO.

"My first thought was, 'Fuck you,'" Jobs told biographer Walter Isaacson. "But then I thought about it and realized that everybody helped me when I was young, from Bill Hewlett to the guy down the block who worked for HP. So I called him back and said sure."

And to his credit, Page was able to hear difficult words from Silicon Valley's foremost legend. Google had been utilizing a "let a thousand flowers bloom" approach, allowing its developers considerable latitude in the projects they undertook, and hoping that some of them would be revolutionary."

Jobs pushed back on Google's fundamental approach. "The main thing I stressed was focus," Jobs said. "Figure out what Google wants to be when it grows up. It's now all over the map. What are the five products you want to focus on? Get rid of the rest, because they're dragging you down. They're turning you into Microsoft. They're causing you to turn out products that are adequate but not great." And the result was a sort of diffusing of the company's energies.

Page was able to learn while also remaining confident in his own judgment. Not long after his conversation with Jobs, Page would tell investors on a quarterly earnings call that Google would be narrowing its focus and "putting more wood behind fewer arrows." Page would go on to win praise from skeptics in the media and the business world: No one had doubted his genius. But they had doubted his ability to learn and to adjust course.

# FOUR

## YOU NEED TO LET GO OF WHAT YOU'RE NOT GOOD AT

SCENARIO A: You're a great actor—
and a lousy director.

**THE ROAD TO HELL:** You may be charismatic, you may enjoy attention, and many people may enjoy you—but you may still be a mediocre manager, unskilled at follow-through, handling budgets or making tough decisions. This thankless task of leadership is giving you an upset stomach and contempt for most of humanity. But you do it anyway because you're convinced that you need the glory of being an "important leader."

**THE ROAD OUT OF HELL:** You realize that you can have more impact, and more satisfaction, by dropping out of management. You can be the actor on the screen, not the migraine-addled director; a cable news pundit instead of a public servant who needs to be held accountable; a Nobel-winning researcher instead of a university president; or any number of high-profile jobs that won't ruin your day and other people's days.

SCENARIO B: You're a great director,
but you're not the best actor.

**THE ROAD TO HELL:** You're great at behind-the-scenes work, but you're not at your best when you're the face of the organization (and most of your employees are afraid to confirm your instincts about this).

**THE ROAD OUT OF HELL:** You do yourself and your organization a huge favor and delegate out many of the public aspects of leadership to gifted emcees, comedians and jugglers.

### Leading Isn't Everything

Alan is a brilliant man. And Alan is a manager. But Alan is not a brilliant manager.

Just because you're wise, brilliant or knowledgeable doesn't mean you should be someone else's boss. Your employees may need to be liberated from you, and you may need to be liberated from the illusion that your importance to the world is linked to the number of people who report to you.

This simple truth is a stumbling block for talented people. They believe that "being gifted" means "rising to the top" or "being in charge," thinking explicitly in *management* terms.

But there are very different ways to rise to the top of your profession. Let's look at a few:

| Occupation | Management Peak | Performance Peak |
|---|---|---|
| Engineer | CEO of Northrop Grumman Corp. | National Academy of Engineering member |
| Actor | Studio executive | Oscar winner |
| Physician | Hospital administrator | Star surgeon or cancer researcher |
| Economics professor | University president | Nobel laureate |
| Writer | Editor-in-chief | Pulitzer winner |

People in the middle row may have great prestige, visibility and power. Frequently, they're drowning in trivia and minutiae. Just as frequently, they're embattled and embroiled in public controversy, turf battles and demands for their resignation or indictment. And quite often, they're dismissed by others as prostitutes who've sold out their professional purity for bottom-line considerations.

## Reality Check

Take a look at the breakdown of responsibilities for your average CEO:

| | |
|---|---|
| Meetings | 40% |
| Vision | 25% |
| Hiring | 20% |
| Managing | 40% |
| Firing | 20% |
| Crisis management | 35% |
| Budgets | 20% |
| Family | 30% |
| Personal growth | 10% |
| Health & fitness | 10% |
| | 250% |

Something doesn't quite add up, does it? It takes a Superman to be a functioning CEO and a deity to be a good one. More often than not, the aspiring CEO believes he's a bit of a deity, which is why he thinks his natural place in the scheme of things is at the very top. But he usually hasn't counted the cost; he typically hasn't done an honest accounting of the pros and cons of leadership.

Herman Wells, the former president of the Indiana University, said that the ideal leader would have "the physical strength of a Greek athlete, the cunning of a Machiavelli, the wisdom of Solomon, the courage of a lion, the skin of a rhino and the stomach of a goat."

That's part of it. He or she should also have the patience of Mother Teresa, the charm of Cleopatra, the eloquence of Shakespeare and the stage presence of Elvis Presley.

But there is no such thing as an ideal leader. Instead, imperfect people seize or inherit or get dragged into the role of leader.

This brings us back to a central issue: *Don't try to lead people unless you actually have some place to lead them.*

If you've been trying to lead people because you thought that the glory of leadership just somehow becomes you, you probably already are beginning to feel chewed up by demands that you never noticed from an idealized distance. That's the safe distance from which you harshly used to judge other people who were in charge, before you began to notice the complexities and limitations and awful win-lose tradeoffs involved in so much leadership.

One of the purposes of this book is to inspire you to ask yourself, about every 15 minutes, "Do I really want to be a manager?" Another purpose is to help you feel good about yourself if your honest answer is "maybe not." The remaining purposes are to help you find the healthiest and most productive way of managing if it's indeed your destiny.

## If You *Must* Lead

Let's imagine that you've considered the matter carefully and have nevertheless decided that management is for you. (Or perhaps you've been pushed into the deep end of the management pool against your will and better judgment—and now you need to know how to tread water.)

Your first goal is to admit that you can't do it all, or at least can't do it all particularly well.

Let's speak of the crucial difference between managers and actors/stars. To be one is not necessarily to be the other.

## Scorsese Leaders: Better Behind the Camera Than in Front of It

Consider a common issue: you may be great at the behind-the-scenes work, directing events like Martin Scorsese directs a film, but you may be less equipped to serve as the public face for your organization. (After all, no one's ever accused Martin Scorsese of having a camera-worthy face.)

This is a conundrum. Given that most leaders' and would-be leaders' egos are overinflated, it's hard for them to imagine that they could be lacking in this "starring" role, which is the one most often associated with being a leader.

Take the case of Larry Page and Sergey Brin, the brainy and geeky founders of Google. Google their names (or Bing them, to level the playing field a little) and you'll find videos of them speaking at various events, usually a bit hesitantly. They are more skilled as directors than actors.

After a while, the company began to offer other spokespersons, such as Eric Schmidt, Marissa Mayer and Nikesh Arora. Page even handed his CEO job over to Schmidt for many years, heeding the suggestions of investors who wanted the then fledgling company to have a more established, "adult" face. Mayer, a photogenic, whip-smart figure, was able to eventually parlay her visibility into the CEO role at languishing competitor Yahoo, and Arora was frequently mentioned as a candidate for that post or similar ones.

Page and Brin allowed themselves to benefit from the skills of others on their team, while simultaneously grooming the next generation of leaders. That was admirable but also shrewdly practical.

Jim Collins' notion of Level 5 managers, in his book *Good to Great*, comes into play here. Level 5 leaders, he argued, are the ones who are best suited to take an organization from good to elite status. As for Scorsese-style managers, Collins said, they tend to be low-key figures rather than celebrities, driven by passion and vision and an attention to detail. They are not entertainers.

## DiCaprio Leaders: Good at the Podium, Bad in the Boardroom

Now consider the flip side. Many people rise to leadership positions because they have a Leonardo DiCaprio quality: they clean up nicely, they present an idea well, and they seize an audience's attention. But they may be woefully weak at the nuts and bolts of management.

We shouldn't completely underestimate how valuable their "face" skills can be. General George C. Marshall once commented that, that "a leader in a democracy must also be an entertainer." He took the matter too far, though. Jim Collins' Level 5 leaders refute the idea that non-entertainers can't lead.

If a person is simply an outstanding actor (as is often the case with politicians), without an ounce of directorial skill, she may not be able to succeed in a leadership role for a particularly long time. Her organization may stagnate or rot from within, or a mutiny may result from followers who demand more competence and less charisma. She could not realistically delegate out the directorial duties to a lieutenant because she wouldn't possess the minimal threshold of directorial skills to judge the effectiveness of the lieutenant. She would be the last to know if the organization were undergoing irreversible decline.

However, if she has a modicum of directorial skill, she will be in a position to delegate out many of the directorial duties to the right person—to a chief of staff, a chief operating officer, or some other key assistant. This celebrity type of leader must learn to cherish the role of the impresario, the one who shrewdly rolls out the best talent for each situation, knowing that in many cases it's not her!

An internationally renowned preacher served as the senior pastor of a historic West Coast Presbyterian church. For years, the congregation thrived, nourished by his popularity and by his compelling vision for his church and his community. Eventually, however, the limitations of his management style became more pronounced. His congregants began clamoring for a real pastor to shepherd them in times of trial, as opposed to a celebrity who was frequently off giving speeches or promoting books in other cities. They began to doubt that his existing team of assistant pastors had the wherewithal to navigate the uncertainties of shrinking budgets and changing demographics.

The senior pastor did not shed his public celebrity role nor scurry into retirement—nor would that have been effective or necessary, considering his role as the beloved patriarch of the church and a revered national figure. Instead, he recruited the best executive pastor he could find, and commissioned him to be the sort of personal and administrative presence that he wasn't able to be. It took a combination of clear-headedness and humility to shift to this approach, which resulted in years of stability and growth for the church.

## Icarus Leaders: Those Who Make Better Number 2s than Number 1s

Let's surmise, somewhat unscientifically that 25 percent of leaders have egos that are underinflated,

5 percent have egos that are inflated "just right," while 70 percent have egos that are overinflated.

Just as the overinflation tendency makes it hard for managers and aspiring leaders to consider that they shouldn't be in charge of others, it makes it almost impossible for them to consider that they may be better off as a vice president than a president. They end up trying to fly too high, usually with awful results.

Norm Chow may have been the best and most accomplished offensive coordinator in the history of college football, especially based on his tenures at BYU and USC, where he shaped teams that won national championships and Heisman trophies. He personally mentored and developed quarterbacks such as Jim McMahon, Steve Young, Philip Rivers, Ty Detmer, Carson Palmer, and Matt Leinart. But Chow was haunted for years by the siren song of the CEO position. He wasn't content to be the world's most valuable Number 2, and continually broadcasted his desire to be a head coach.

It was news to no one but Chow that he wasn't a good fit for a head coaching gig. At the college football level, a head coach must be a tireless recruiter, a constant wooer of alumni and journalists, and a thick-skinned lightning rod for criticism. Chow wasn't naturally any of those. At an advanced stage of his career, he continued to distract himself with real and perceived head coaching opportunities with the Arizona Cardinals in the NFL as well as Stanford, UCLA, North Carolina State and Kentucky at the college level. All this restlessness ended up diminishing his platform and record as an offensive coordinator. He soon spiraled downward to the unglamorous job of offensive coordinator at the University of Utah.

When he finally got his chance at a head coaching job at the age of 65, in 2012, at the University of Hawaii, his team earned an unimpressive 3-9 record. It made many observers wonder how much more he could have achieved if he had focused on his offensive specialty, which had allowed him to focus on mentoring legendary college quarterbacks and state-of-the-art offenses.

Tex Winter went in the opposite direction from Chow. Winter was a head basketball coach for years at the college level at schools like Kansas State and the University of Washington, and even spent a few years as head coach of the NBA's Houston Rockets. He was modestly successful in the head role.

In 1985, at the age of 63, Winter agreed to serve as an assistant coach for the Chicago Bulls, which would give him a chance to mentor a promising young athlete who happened to be named Michael Jordan. In 1989, Phil Jackson would take over as the Bulls' head coach, and Winter was willing to work alongside Jackson, focusing on his specialty: installing and improving the "Triangle" offensive system that Winter had himself designed.

This allowed Winter to accumulate six championship rings as an assistant for the Bulls and three rings later as Jackson's key assistant with the Los Angeles Lakers (Winter would be an 87-year-old Lakers consultant for a 10th title).

By finding his right level as a manager, Winter achieved his greatest professional impact. In addition to the glory of the 10 championship rings, he received the Chuck Daly Lifetime Achievement Award from the NBA Coaches Association in 2010, and a year later would be inducted into the Naismith Basketball Hall of Fame.

## DiCaprio Leaders = Paper Bag Leaders

DiCaprio Leaders can be thought of as paper bag leaders, given how they are charismatic and mesmerizing yet lacking key management skills. Despite their charm, they never actually are able to lead their way out of a damp paper bag.

There are a number of duties that most every manager must perform. If he isn't naturally skilled at them, he must develop a certain minimal competency in them while being willing and ready to place much of those duties in the hands of a capable lieutenant.

**1. Hiring duties.** The leader ideally has a nose for real talent and the ability to sniff out poseurs and sycophants. The charismatic leader often fails here, because he can be won over by hacks who talk a good game or who excel only at the dark art of flattery.

Paper-bag leaders tend to make the following mistakes:

**The paper bag leader confuses pedigree with talent.**

It seems impressive to hire a person with a background from an Ivy League school or other highly selective institution. We like bragging that we just brought in some hotshot from a name-brand school. These persons are the best and the brightest, right?

Not necessarily. A person may attend elite private elementary and secondary schools that help her graduate with honors from Brown. But that does not mean that she's as much of an achiever as someone who had the deck stacked against her but who fought her way to graduate from the local state college. The branding of an elite college grad is more effective than it should be, and this prevents many jewels in the rough from being discovered. More to the point, loading up on Ivy League grads may be counterproductive, because you don't know enough about what they're made of. That leads to the next mistake.

**The paper bag leader hasn't trained his eye to spot beach balls.**

Next time you're at the beach or a swimming pool, try submerging a beach ball completely under water. It's exhausting just to try to hold it down, isn't it? Many people are like beach balls—they'll rise up, no matter what the circumstance. They're the opposite of people who "coulda been a contender" if only all the stars had aligned. These people don't make excuses for why their life had disappointments, and they don't blame bosses or colleagues for keeping them from reaching their potential. That comes out soon enough in an interview.

Their resume offers signs of their irresistible upward push. While some gifted gabbers can indefinitely keep parlaying a good job at one company into a better job at another company, (until they come up against the Peter Principle) the beach ball has a consistent habit of being rewarded with more responsibility within the same department or organization.

These people also often have outside interests, and show a similar tendency to be handed extra responsibilities in those other voluntary capacities. They typically emerge as the indispensable leaders or key lieutenants in any career-related or volunteer endeavor. Usually their references are willing to say that about them. If no reference makes such an observation, take that as a cautionary sign.

**The paper bag leader knows only the conventional way to measure intelligence.**

Psychologist and science writer Daniel Goleman stood management on its head several years ago when he articulated his theories of "emotional intelligence." Contrary to traditional belief, Goleman held that only a third of a person's success could be attributed to her IQ and technical expertise. A baseline of intelligence gets you in the game, Goleman said, but up to two-thirds of a person's career success derived from her "emotional intelligence"—her ability to get along with other people, read other people, and move other people in new directions.

Evidence of Goleman's rightness isn't hard to find. It's the reason that "dumb" politicians regularly win elections over colder eggheaded politicians, here in a democracy that's supposed to know better but which chooses to have a beer with the dumb guy anyway. It's the reason that many young brainiac tech executives crash against the rocks once their decision-making algorithms are pitted against the unfathomable mysteries of consumer and investor behavior.

Google recently stopped asking prospective employees for their SAT scores, even if they're 20 years out of college. This has some real value, given how SATs are supposed to measure aptitude. But as Malcolm Gladwell pointed out in *Outliers*, standardized tests are "convergence tests"—they require you to converge on one narrow answer out of multiple choices. In essence, that measures and rewards conformity.

A divergence test, on the other hand, tests a person's creativity, through questions such as, "How many uses can you come up with for a brick? For a blanket?" How many times were you tested and rewarded in school for that ability? Not many, of course. Yet divergent thinking is incredibly important to any company, especially in a place such as Silicon Valley, where constant change demands vision and creativity within the talent base. This is one reason for the expression, "the MFA is the new MBA." Imagination matters more than ever.

Raw IQ alone isn't enough. Charisma alone isn't enough. An outstanding academic pedigree alone isn't enough. In some cases, these traits may be unnecessary and counterproductive. True talent must be measured in ways that are contrary to most conventional management wisdom.

**2. Firing duties.** The leader needs to know when to be patient with an underachiever and when to fire the underachiever, for the good of both the organization and the underachiever.

Organizations have many reasons for underachieving: managers can't agree on a strategy, managers can't agree on priorities or managers are unready for twists along the economic landscape. But the most glaring reason for underperformance is that most managers stink at the art of dismissing underperformers.

The economic and human costs are huge. Organizations stagnate when managers are too timid to ease out employees who are underperforming—and these employees resent the palpable sense that they're not appreciated, which leads to sniping that yanks morale down further. Worst of all, a culture of non-accountability builds. It benefits everyone if the civilized art of "employee liberation" is cultivated.

Here are some ways in which paper-bag leaders err in this area:

**The paper bag leader believes that under-performers need his charity.**

Too often, these managers suspect they're performing an act of compassion by keeping underperformers on the payroll. They should ask shareholders, voters or other stakeholders to which they're beholden whether that charity is appropriate. They should ask high-achieving colleagues if they feel such charity to underachievers is appropriate. Just as importantly, a manager would do an underperformer a favor if she instead gave him a new lease on his career, at a place that might be a better match for his talents.

In one corporation, a senior manager had little faith in the ability of a middle manager but was too kind (or too cowardly) to terminate him. Instead, she moved him around from one department to the next over two years, while hiring new staff to compensate for his deficiencies. He in turn, understandably, felt unappreciated. When she finally dismissed him after having had enough, he turned around and filed suit. Consider her mistakes here. She bloated the organization's headcount irresponsibly; she failed to give him the proper feedback in real time that could have allowed him to make peace with the notion that he was a bad fit at the company; and she treated him too long like a charity case, which only increased his resentment and readiness to sue.

**The paper bag leader fails to define success clearly and early.**

Your organization won't value you for just staying in place. It will value you as a manager if you raise productivity or quality in your area. It's up to you to define what that looks like. And if you can do so, for yourself and your employees, you now have clear, guilt-free parameters for addressing underperformance.

**When ready to take action, the paper bag leader doesn't give adequate warning.**

There may be times when a firing has to be sudden. But for the most part, human beings resent the idea of the ambush firing or layoff. In companies, the "human" in "human resources" often yields to the "law" in "lawyer." This is understandable. But in too many cases, this leads to managers only having the guts to fire an underperformer for an irrelevant technicality rather than for the actual underperformance. If a valuable employee gets caught Facebooking during regular work hours, in a violation of company policy, her violation will likely be quietly reprimanded or ignored altogether. If a ne'er-do-well does the same, he may get canned. This approach is cowardly, as it allows expedience to take the place of honest discussion about overall performance issues.

In most cases, I've had good relations and friendships with those whom I've had to move out the door, mainly because they knew it was nothing personal—just a matter of them and our organization being better served by a change.

I used to believe that nonprofits aren't as effective at firing as corporations, because corporations are more ruthlessly interested in maximizing profits. I later found that to be untrue; a classic example was a friend's public relations firm, which organized workshops instructing managers on why never to fire employees, lest the firm get dragged into court.

**3. Fiscal duties.** The charismatic, paper bag leader often deludes himself and his followers into believing that their organization will somehow magically rise out of debt by tapping new donors or new markets.

Here is how paper bag leaders bungle this area:

**The paper bag leader says, "Trust me."**

I worked with the governing body of a large and historic church, where I watched one such leader argue that, if only the congregation obeyed his direction and had faith, God would imminently bless the church with new people and new funds. He was not necessarily a charlatan; he was probably sincere in his own beliefs. Nevertheless, he was terrible with budgets, and the church soon fell $1 million in debt.

A critical mass of doubters arose who demanded fiscal discipline in addition to faith. What ensued was a painful civil war within the church, featuring harsh words and accusations on all sides. To the bitter end, the failing pastor insisted that God was on his side. But better budget skills would have helped too. As it turned out, he was driven out of a prestigious, high-profile dream job, and he struggled in ensuing years to rebuild any kind of credible following or ministry.

**The paper-bag leader blames it all on a lack of money.**

Most middle and upper-middle managers fall into this quagmire. They lament, "The CEO wants me to move heaven and earth, but she won't give me the budget for the bulldozers and the construction equipment."

This typically betrays a lack of entrepreneurialism, imagination or courage. Many a middle manager has had his wings clipped on his ascent because of this shortcoming. Every healthy organization wants managers who believe they can make the weather or at least survive the weather; they don't want managers who submit requests for more umbrellas.

Again, a good amount of these skills can be delegated to lieutenants, with some big ifs, as in 1) if the leader has enough understanding of these areas to determine whether those lieutenants are succeeding, and 2) if the leader has enough wherewithal to replace them if they're not succeeding. Bear in mind that the second point is no given!

# FIVE

## YOU'RE TRYING TO PROVE YOURSELF, INSTEAD OF JUST EXPRESSING YOURSELF

**THE ROAD TO HELL:** You're on a desperate quest for respect. You don't know the Zen of playfully getting lost in what you love, without regard for outcomes. You feel your life won't be complete until people in distant lands adore you. You find yourself more invested in people you can't touch or see than the people right in front of you. Your own family and friends get a small fraction of your care, because you know you can't be worshipped adequately by the people who have seen your neurotic side at Thanksgiving dinner.

**THE ROAD OUT OF HELL:** You invest as much (or more) energy in the human beings in your life as you do with people you'll never meet. Your goal is to express yourself, not to prove yourself. When you die, the saddest people at your funeral will be the ones who knew you closely, not the ones who didn't know you beyond the face on a screen.

The ancient Zen masters understood a fundamental aspect of high performance: To achieve her best, a person must be in a state of play, *not* a state of anxiety.

Being determined has some advantages, but being too determined has only disadvantages. If I throw a tennis ball toward you, you can only catch it if you relax your fingers and palm. Make them rigid and grasping, and the ball will bounce off your hand to the floor.

The person who plays best is often one who plays at what he loves, for the love of the game.

Leadership experts today have found just what the Zen masters did: a good, healthy, self-actualized leader is driven by the same healthy impulses as a top athlete who loses himself in a state of play. Warren Bennis summarized it best when he observed in *On Becoming a Leader* that the difference between many good leaders and bad leaders is that **good leaders seek to express themselves, while bad leaders seek to prove themselves.**

Shaquille O'Neal was physically the most dominant specimen in the history of basketball, with monstrous size and surprising agility. Most basketball experts would agree that he was one of the 10 best players in the history of the sport. Yet most would also agree that he left many more championships and individual honors unclaimed. This is because Shaq played the game mainly to prove himself, not to express his love for the game. When called out by critics, he would respond with a 60-point performance. When comfortable with himself, he would go soft and add excessive weight to his massive frame. He was fun-loving, but not loving the fun of competition as much as loving the chance to be a ham for the cameras and journalists. Eventually, his lack of commitment to excellence led to fallouts with a number of teams. Occasionally, he would round himself into shape, but usually just to prove doubters wrong.

Why is the difference between expressing yourself and proving yourself important for a leader?

A person driven largely by a need for respect will only be able to show up occasionally, when sufficiently outraged—and for only as long as doubters are making themselves heard. For Shaq, this prevented him from achieving maximum performance over the long haul.

In most cases, the person who is seeking to prove himself goes too far, for too long, and never feels he has actually proved himself. He never silences those haunting voices of doubt. And eventually he ends up in the position of Icarus, foolishly flying too high and tumbling to earth as a result.

The good leader does what he does as a natural, organic expression of his values and his convictions. The bad leader does what he does to earn respect, to quiet voices in his head. This leader may well succeed in the short term, but he is the one who will lose his internal compass, go too far, ride off a cliff and take others with him.

Jeffrey Skilling and Ken Lay of Enron would be primary exhibits of this latter kind of leadership. Consider the reality that they, for years, were the toast of the business world. Business and news magazines could not help but erect literary monuments to their excellence. They were described as "the smartest people in the room," and they took pride in that billing.

They played the energy distribution game shrewdly and frantically in order to generate money, success and headlines. Later, they needed to play it even more shrewdly and frantically, to sustain their momentum on the nightmarish hamster wheel of success that they had engineered. Eventually, the wheel broke off and crashed. More than $1 billion in wealth disappeared, much of that in the form of vanished pension funds of loyal workers who took pride in being a part of a great American success story.

## Cradles of Eminence, Nurseries of Misery

"When the work is done, and one's name is becoming distinguished, to withdraw into obscurity is the way of Heaven," Lao Tzu said in the classic *Tao Te Ching*.

Lao Tzu cautioned leaders that the only sane and healthy way of doing one's job is 1) to just do it, and 2) to let go of the results. There is a case to be made that leaders who can do this leave the most positive mark, with the least collateral damage or unintended consequences.

But letting go of the results is the hardest thing to do for most of the ambitious people who gravitate toward leadership positions. The results are the only thing that matter to them.

The landmark book, *Cradles of Eminence*, examined 700 famous persons and found a common theme. From Mother Teresa to Hitler to Gandhi to Stalin, they were malcontents, which made each of them obsessed with "making a dent in the universe," to use the words of the ever-active, ever-dreaming but ever-unsatisfied Steve Jobs. Deciding to put a dent in the universe may well be the fastest way to put a dent in your own happiness — and the happiness of the people around you.

## The Obvious Downside to "Never Being Satisfied"

Jobs was canonized for what he was able to achieve and what he was able to change, due to his uncompromising, restless, "never be satisfied" approach. But the only problem with never being satisfied is that, surprisingly, you'll never be satisfied. Jobs went to his grave with a pile of accomplishments and a long list of grievances. My own suspicion is that if he'd lived to 90, he might have been unhappy, because he'd have lived long enough to see his industry and his legacy and his peers go in directions he couldn't hope to control.

As noted earlier, Jobs makes a complicated role model for leaders and would-be leaders. While many of them aspire to be *viewed like* Jobs, the question is whether they want to *be like* Jobs. Jobs had a petty streak, besmirched many employees' dignity for less than noble reasons and gave short shrift to some of the most important people in his life. His career was a Faustian bargain of sorts.

Further consider that Jobs was successful in no small part because he had perhaps a one-in-a-billion combination of vision, passion and luck, all galvanized by the ghosts that haunted a child uncomfortable with his place in the world. In the spirit of *Cradles of Eminence*, a person unsure of his place in the universe is going to feel an obsessive need to make a dent in it, just to convince himself that he exists.

Even if Jobs' track record was available to you, would you necessarily believe it was the best thing for every leader? With luck and a lot of sacrifice, you just might make a Jobsian dent in the universe, but the universe is bigger than you, and it will leave some sizable dents in you as well.

The Steve Jobs approach worked well enough for one person—Steve Jobs. And it's debatable whether he was happy at last, or whether he might have made a better impact on our world if he brought a different perspective.

**Proving Yourself as a Faustian Bargain: Michael Jordan**

Is there a curse attached to Michael Jordan's success?

The issue has arisen now and then, as Jordan has slid into an awkward and restless middle age. This was symbolized best by him offering up the most uncharitable Hall of Fame acceptance speech ever in 2009, a snide bashing of former colleagues that served notice that the chip on his shoulder was as permanent a part of his anatomy as his lungs.

Sportswriter J.A. Adande would later chalk it up this way: "Jordan spoke from the heart. The thing is, his heart's as cold as liquid nitrogen. ... You don't get his triumphing again and again without his using every slight—real or perceived—to motivate himself." Adande noted that other honorees that night (including David Robinson and John Stockton) were humble and self-deprecating, offering "an unmistakable thread of peace of mind and purpose." Jordan by contrast, was "oddly insecure."

Author Lane Wallace, writing for TheAtlantic.com a few years later, observed that, as a child, "the young Jordan believed his father preferred his older brother, and spent a lifetime driven to achieve as a way of proving his worth. ... Hence the drive, the rage, the relentless pursuit of victory that led to astounding feats of skill and six championship rings in his dresser drawer."

But a person who gives himself permission to prove himself at all costs will make the first available deal with the devil.

Jordan would admit to ESPN.com that those rings came at a cost. "You ask for these special powers to achieve these heights, and now you got it and you want to give it back, but you can't. ... I drove myself so much that I'm still living with some of those drives. ... I don't know how to get rid of it."

Shaq and Jordan both played basketball to prove themselves. Shaq did it in spurts, whereas Jordan did it constantly. Jordan achieved a level of on-court performance Shaq never did, but his success came with its own downside—which is that few people seemingly would have anything to do with him if he didn't have his particular highlight reel.

Wallace tellingly suggested that the demons that possessed Jordan also own many leaders in other realms. She recounted a friend's description of your typical CEO: "Almost to a person, they've been denied something that really mattered to them, early in their lives," the friend told her. "So they spend the rest of their lives making up for it. Achieving. And not only does that make them pretty focused on themselves, it also means that no achievement is ever enough."

Let's check back in 10 years and compare how Jordan is doing with how LeBron James is doing. I've personally been a far greater admirer of Jordan than James (After Jordan played in an exhibition game at Pauley Pavilion early in his NBA career, he was swarmed by admirers as he left. I ran up behind him, touched his back like he was Jesus with healing powers, then walked away suspecting I'd have a story I could tell for the rest of my life). James has not been as possessed as Jordan, which is why he, at the time of this writing, may have one or two fewer championship rings than he might have had.

James had been pummeled by critics for being too deferential in the clutch, for not burning with a win-at-all-costs desire. But many have noticed that the upside is that James plays with a purer love for the game than Jordan did. It may well be that James acquits himself better over the long journey of life than Jordan, because his play is an expression of his love for the game rather than an effort to humiliate all real and perceived rivals.

Let's examine, then, how to bring a better perspective. It will strain your emotions and your brain cells, but it's the most important thing you can do in your life.

**Being vs. Doing**

Where do you fall on the *being vs. doing* scale? The healthy and productive leader grasps a number of delicate distinctions between the two. And grasping those distinctions is the key to refining one's motives, to ensure that you're more motivated by a whimsical desire to express yourself than a grim need to prove yourself.

Many philosophers and theologians have argued through the ages that it is healthier to "be" than to "do." The reasoning is that a person should have a strong, unshakable sense of identity that isn't based on how much fantastic work she does or the length of her accomplishments. That sense of identity should come from her being grounded in an unchanging sense of her innate worth, not from a sense of worth that she has temporarily generated through frantic activity.

In this view, a person who focuses too much on "doing" would anxiously perform a never-ending series of hoop-jumps in order to feel substantial. If she were ever to stop doing those hoop-jumps, she would quickly lose her sense of worth. That indeed is a prescription for misery. (As the late Trappist monk Thomas Merton noted, when such unhappy people set out to make the world a better place, they usually just infect it with the contagion of their own unhappiness.)

Once you refine your motivations by putting *being* ahead of *doing*, it's time to shift perspectives. Think about how *doing* can be more satisfying than *being*. As Varun Soni, the dean of religious life at USC and a practicing Hindu, told me, "The advice I give to bright and ambitious students is that it's better to find what you love to do, and to just do it."

As Soni (who once spent a year contemplating life in a Buddhist monastery) sees it, many people want to "be" something—a movie star, a president, a Nobel laureate. But one hitch is that people tend not to become any happier once they achieve such lofty states of "being." Psychologists point to a phenomenon known as "hedonic adaptation," where a temporary additional joy reverts back to an older baseline.

An even more obvious hitch is that, no matter how good they are at their craft, they cannot control whether they become a movie star, a president, a Nobel laureate or even a PTA chairman.

But if they cannot control who they hope to *be*, at a professional or social level, they can control what they *do*. Here Soni argues that it's imperative for a person to find something that she could *love* to do.

## R-E-S-P-E-C-T: Find Out What It Means to *You*

I faced a crossroads in my career a few years ago. The issue was whether to do what I felt I was born to do—which is to write and speak and think for a living—or to do what would give me the greatest amount of respect and income in the short term.

I had a good resume and a great day job as a top communications adviser at a large organization. I had the flexibility to do a great deal of thinking and writing on the side. I even had friends and family telling me I should count my blessings to have it so good during an awful recession.

I had little argument with that. But I also struggled with the internal political battles that had been raging, which led me to believe that I didn't have the support I needed or the respect I deserved from all quarters.

Many a friend and many a colleague told me that, while my situation had its genuine headaches, my blind spot was an inability to affirm the good in my situation. I was too thin-skinned, they told me, and they worried I may react rashly and escape a role that I had worked for years to establish.

## The Road to Hell is Paved with a Veneer of Respectability

I came to my senses, but only after coming very close to being detoured for possibly years, in a new job in a new town that I knew wasn't right for me, but which I would have taken simply to escape feelings of worthlessness that I ultimately was imposing on myself.

If you're a people-pleaser, you'll find it impossible to be content merely expressing yourself. You won't even know what that looks like. You've been too busy sensing what would impress other people, then seeking to do that to the exclusion of everything else.

Too many aspiring leaders foolishly try to find their passion in life while simultaneously making it their highest priority to keep people around them happy. Realistically, they either need to give up on their own dreams or give up on maximizing others' happiness.

I'm not necessarily telling you to give up on pleasing the rest of us. For millennia, whole civilizations have been based on the idea that the individual owes duty to the community more than duty to his own desires.

## An Asian Dilemma: Who Writes Your Script?

Even today, shame-based cultures, ranging from the Middle East to East Asia, tell you that you can't write the script of your life. Instead, they tell you that the script of your life has been written by your family or your tribe or your religion or your government.

If that's convincing or compelling to you, then make peace with it — and bury your own private longings and goals and passions and dreams. Then move on. It doesn't help you or others to pout and to feel obligated to your family or community if you secretly harbor a grudge against them for getting in the way of your own true happiness. They can probably smell resentment on your breath. They can intuitively sense the numbness in your soul as you shuffle your way through a waking death.

Yes, they want you to live the way that they've strongly been suggesting (or even demanding). But they don't want you pointing your finger at them in your last days, condemning them for keeping you from what you wanted to be.

This has been a major theme in my life. I grew up between cultures, as a Pakistani-American. I spent my childhood and much of my adult life listening to people telling me that I "belonged" primarily to Pakistan or America, and that certain duties were implied. I made choices that I frankly thought would make me the detested black sheep of my family. In time, though, my family came to accept my choices.

A painful reality for many people from tradition-bound and community-bound cultures is that, if you do want to live your own life, you are going to have to learn to be a disappointment to those who are closest to you. You are going to have to accept that they won't be happy with you, and learn to be at peace with that. The simple fact is that, if you can learn to be a disappointment, you have a real chance to do what you want to do, go where you want to go, be who you want to be—and lead how you want to lead.

## The Virtue of Being a "Do Nothing"

"But what do I love to do?"

If you're over the age of 30, it becomes more and more difficult to answer that simple question, due to so many decades of listening to others tell you what your goals should be. Sure, you love playing basketball or love hiking, but you can't conceive anyone paying you to do so, because you've frankly seen how much better the competition is.

Learning what you love to do involves some unlearning. Let's call on the sage Lao Tzu again for some puzzling and paradoxical and profound advice from his *Tao Te Ching* ("Tao" represents "the way of heaven").

"Those who possessed [wisdom] in the highest degree did nothing and had no need to do anything" Lao Tzu said in his hallmark philosophy, "Those who possessed them in a lower degree were always doing and had need to be so doing" He also said "It is the way of the Tao to act without thinking of acting; and to conduct affairs without feeling the trouble of them."

Doing nothing, working without effort, or acting without doing, doesn't mean sitting on the couch eating bonbons while the world magically tends to itself. Doing nothing means doing what comes so naturally that it *feels* effortless.

Doing nothing means doing nothing that's contrived, nothing that's forced, nothing that represents a strained and sweaty effort to make a Jobsian dent.

Lao Tzu's Taoist thought would meld with Buddhist thought to sire the enduringly influential Zen approach, in which the practitioner ceases her anxious striving and begins to lose herself in the activity of the moment. Eventually, the practitioner can begin to love a variety of mundane activities, by fully appreciating the moment and letting go of any need to ding up the universe.

By seeking to be in tune with the universe (or "being one with the Tao"), she becomes naturally able to express her distinct personality and talents as a form of play, not labor. Playing a favorite game may seem like doing a whole lot of nothing, but that's what life can be (and should be), as Lao Tzu would have it. It's a form of wisdom that's lost far too often in our workaholic, multitasking age

**The Wallenda Factor**

"The only time I feel truly alive is when I walk the tightrope," aerial artist Karl Wallenda once said. For Wallenda, everything else was just waiting. Waiting for the next chance to feel fully alive.

Warren Bennis distilled an extraordinary leadership metaphor from Wallenda's life, a metaphor that has gained far too little notice within management circles. In an essay some years ago, he noted that Wallenda would fall to his death in 1978, during one of his most dangerous walks. Wallenda's wife would later recall that his focus had seemed to shift in the months preceding the event. For the first time in his career, Wallenda had begun personally supervising the installation of security measures.

"All Karl thought about for about three months straight prior to it was falling," he said. "It was the first time he'd ever thought about that, and it seemed to me that he put all his energy into not falling, not into walking the tightrope."

A great performer would die when he began to focus more on the threat of failure than on the joy of performing. He would lose his life when he worried more about dying than when he worried about doing the one thing that made him feel alive. That is the lesson, for people seeking maximum performance and adventure, in any realm.

An observation by the late clergyman and activist Howard Thurman gets to the issue from a similar angle. "Don't ask what the world needs," Thurman said. "Ask what makes you come alive, and go do it. Because what the world needs is people who have come alive."

## Time to Play Ball

"Happy, well-adjusted people don't try to take over the world," Laura Harbert, a gifted psychologist in Monterey, California once told me. "They put in an honest day's work—and then they go home and toss the ball around with the kids."

It's the unhappy, poorly adjusted people who feel a combination of inspiration and torment that pushes them to stay late at the office, in their quest to climb ever higher. The kid won't have a parent to throw the ball around with, but the kid will surely understand that it's for his or her own good, the climber reasons. But it's not for no reason that climbers typically confess, later in life, that they wish they'd spent less time at the office and more time with their children during those key shaping moments.

## Phony Relationships and the Dilemma of Fame

I'd heard a story years ago about a Hollywood legend before he became legendary. A friend had taken an acting class with this young man, who was constantly propositioning the women in the class. He had no success—and no one was surprised, because his personal hygiene was atrocious. It was no treat to be asked out by this actor, but most every actress in the class was forced to deal diplomatically with this rite of passage.

A few years later, fate gave him his opportunity. He cleaned up enough to become one of Hollywood's most desirable men. Women fought over him. Interestingly, it has been said that his hygiene never actually improved. But it became less of a factor, as women were willing to hold their noses to be in his presence.

This raises the issue of authenticity: Do people love the leader (or the celebrity or any type of heroic figure) because of the person's qualities, or because of the mystique and hype that has become attached to that person or to that person's job title?

The purpose of such questions is to help current and aspiring leaders clarify their motivations—and to refine them in any possible way. When a person sets out to "prove" himself, he typically uses popularity and glory to measure his success. Yet in most cases, the popularity he enjoys is largely among a faceless mass of people who do not know the real person; he is simply a projection of their own psychological needs for hero worship.

**The Bottom Line**

People who want to be leaders don't necessarily want to accomplish a certain objective. They often just want to be the hero.

Yet one great truth is that it is hard to be a hero to people who know you too well. It is easier to be a hero to people on distant continents or future generations, who will never encounter the less heroic side that all of us possess in ample measure.

The second great truth comes in the words of Ralph Waldo Emerson: "Every hero becomes a bore at last." Eventually the hero who is worshipped in spite of himself and his hygiene becomes old news.

That is why a would-be leader is courting frustration and futility if he seeks the leadership position solely to puff up his ego, rather than as a means to accomplish a specific purpose. Here we return to Lao Tzu's advice at the beginning of this chapter: "When the work is done, and one's name is becoming distinguished, to withdraw into obscurity is the way of Heaven."

A major benefit of this approach is that the leader begins to become more present to the people in his life. That means he has a chance, at his funeral, to be mourned even more by those who really knew him than by those who didn't know him. For most leaders, the sad and futile reality is that it is the other way around.

**No Easy Answers**

Give yourself a break. There are people you may look up to and idolize, but precious few of them didn't question the worth or impact of their careers, even on their deathbeds.

There are no easy answers. This chapter may have reawakened in you that gnawing dream of being an actor instead of a financial consultant, or a sailor instead of a vice principal. You're thus wrestling once again between whether to serve a crazy passion or common sense.

There is no obvious answer to the question. The point is to be honest with yourself, and to make peace with your answers.

We mentioned the Simon Cowell factor in an earlier chapter. What if a Simon Cowell-type of figure told you that your acting was mediocre and that you could earn a lot more money by sticking to your financial consulting day job? Would you listen to the voice of a Cowell? Or might you instead heed a quiet voice inside that tells you to keep pursuing your dream?

While there are no easy answers, there are right ways to ask the question. The question isn't "Do you want to be a famous and successful actor?" The question is rather, "Do you love acting?" The question isn't "Would you do anything to be a famous actor?" but rather, "Are you willing to make some financial sacrifices in order to wake up each morning with the chance to do something you *like* to do—even if it's just community theater that requires you to work part-time as a Starbucks barista?"

# SIX

## YOU THINK, DEEP DOWN, THAT IT REALLY MIGHT BE ALL ABOUT YOU

**THE ROAD TO HELL:** You treat life as if all eyes are supposed to be on you, even though you know that you're not supposed to be seen as a blowhard egotist.

**THE ROAD OUT OF HELL:** You treat life as if you're the world's most skilled talk show host, helping everyone to shine and have a good time.

The Western mind thinks of leadership in terms of statues: A great man performs great feats, which stirs others to think of him in grandiose terms. To honor the man, we erect a larger than life symbol of him, and his legend grows—even while various detractors complain that he "got lucky" or that his misdeeds have been conveniently swept aside.

Little has changed to this day, save for the notion that the great man may be a woman, and that a certain percentage of statues that are erected should be of women. This is progress, yes, but it misses something.

### Rise and Fall of the Gladstonians

William Gladstone and Benjamin Disraeli were two of England's most renowned prime ministers of the 19th century. Both had distinguished careers, but the two contrasted considerably in style.

As some say the story went, when you had dinner with William Gladstone, you left nodding your head, thinking, "That William Gladstone is the wittiest, the most intelligent, and the most charming person around!"

But when you had dinner with Benjamin Disraeli, you left nodding your head, thinking, "I am the wittiest, the most intelligent, and the most charming person around!"

Gladstone had many gifts, which allowed him to shine forth brightly before men. But Disraeli had a special gift of drawing out the best in others, so that they could shine.

An "all about me" leader could counter, "Yes, but can you really make the case that Disraeli achieved any more than Gladstone did?"

First, let's consider a moral response. When most people hear the Gladstone/Disraeli parable, their idealistic impulses take wing. Their spirit resonates profoundly with the notion that the leader should be in it for others, not for herself.

### Gladstonians Won't Prosper for Long in a Disraelian World

Then there is a pragmatist's response: The Disraeli way is the inherently democratic way, and while our world is becoming more democratic every day his way will yield greater results in coming years.

Fareed Zakaria's must-read 2003 book, *The Future of Freedom*, illustrated how the democratization of institutions globally means that the traditional experts and elites and authorities have less sway than ever over the masses. Think about it: Measures of success are now tied to clicks, eyeballs, sales rankings and aggregated user rankings. We pay less attention to what a small group of experts pronounces to be good or bad. More than ever, the Simon Cowells of the world offer commentary, but the ultimate judges are ordinary people.

A powerful Gladstonian could get his way within a democratic organization more easily in the past and could intimidate dissenters and skeptics. Today those with skeptical voices can control the conversation through the Internet, mobile technologies and social media more effectively than the Gladstonian can.

There is at least one other practical reason to favor the Disraeli way. The person who walks out of Disraeli's home feels better about herself, quite possibly realizing talents in herself that she had not noticed before Disraeli praised them. Such a person becomes attached to the Disraeli-style leader at a deeper level than the hero-worship associated with the Gladstone-style leader.

You know examples of the Disraeli way in your own life. I recall hearing the management guru Charles Handy speak at a conference honoring one of my chief mentors, Warren Bennis. Handy spoke of Warren's uncanny ability to look deeply into the eyes of whomever was speaking to him, as if to say, "You, my friend, are the most interesting person on the planet." The audience, filled with colleagues from around the world, laughed with immediate recognition. (Naturally I laughed too, while also feeling slightly crestfallen to find out that I wasn't the only person he did that to.)

Mark Twain recalled that Disraeli spirit in his own mother, and noted that this spirit preserved her through various infirmities:

> She had a slender, small body but a large heart—a heart so large that everybody's grief and everybody's love found welcome in it and hospitable accommodation. The greatest

difference which I find between her and the rest of the people whom I have know is this, and it is a remarkable one: those others felt a strong interest in a few things, whereas to the very day of her death she felt a strong interest in the whole world and everybody in it.

## HOW IT WORKS IN PRACTICE

When things are going well, the Gladstonian leader seems invincible. But when things change for the worse, the Gladstonian has a lower reserve of goodwill or loyalty to fall back on. In our hyper-democratic era, that means a longtime leader can quickly be out on the street.

During Michael Eisner's tenure at Disney, the legendary company underwent a renaissance. Stock prices and profits soared, as did the brawling and politicking.

During that era, I came upon someone who worked in Disney's accounting unit. I said, "Here's a chance for you to put to death a theory of mine. Disney's supposed to be the happiest place on earth, but I have yet to meet a happy Disney employee."

"Keep looking," he curtly said. Disney was a place to survive for two years, burnish your credentials and then escape with your soul intact.

Disney under Eisner increasingly reflected his combative DNA. He encouraged employees to spar and jockey in Darwinian political struggles. The happiest place on earth was as far from the Disraeli way as one could imagine.

A few months before he was forced into retirement in 2004, *San Francisco Chronicle* business columnist Tim Goodman wrote:

> It's always a bit of a jolt when really powerful people are undone... [T]hat very imperviousness, the I Can Do Anything gene, which made these powerful people who they are, often undoes them.

The all-about-me style of Eisner, accompanied by his force of personality and his genuine vision and talent, worked spectacularly successfully. For a time. Yet it contained within it the seeds of its own demise, in a way that the democratic, inclusive Disraelian style doesn't.

## Clinton vs. Obama vs. Clinton

Let's be clear. Both Gladstone and Disraeli had egos. Neither ego was underinflated. The difference is that the Disraeli style blends a healthy ego with a commitment to getting others in on the fun.

A comparison of Barack Obama and Bill Clinton would suggest that Obama has the Gladstonian streak and Clinton the Disraeli-esque streak. Both were outstanding as orators, but Obama brought more messiah-like praise, especially during his early years of political ascendancy. Obama speeches were considered historic occasions, and his choice of words and images struck admirers as Lincolnian in import and eloquence. Clinton was more folksy and long-winded, but he had the ability to make listeners feel as though they were in his living room, chatting with him about some of the subjects that he just couldn't get enough of.

Observers have said that, when Clinton looks at a person, they have his fullest attention and appreciation; he will even maintain unbroken eye contact while drinking a glass of water by looking at the other person through the bottom of a water glass. Former aide Paul Begala noted that Clinton gives everyone he meets a smile and a warm hug. (Indeed, we know that his capacity to seduce voters went a bit far on occasion.)

By comparison, observers have found Obama to be cool and detached, almost Vulcan-like. One former Obama adviser who also worked under Hillary Clinton offered an intriguing contrast between Mrs. Clinton and Obama: "Hillary Clinton wasn't great in front of a microphone on a big stage. Her personality almost seemed to shrink. But in a small room, she'd light up, and she'd connect with everyone in that room. Obama lights up when he's in front of a microphone at a rally or major event. But he becomes kind of disconnected when he meets with a small group of people."

That helps us understand what makes Mr. Clinton the most gifted American political leader since Reagan and John F. Kennedy. He did not have the political liabilities that either his wife or his Democratic successor had. Years after his impeachment, he soldiered on as a global philanthropist and pro bono Democratic consultant, boasting higher approval ratings than any other major American political figure.

During Obama's re-election campaign, journalists noted that well-heeled Democratic supporters, who wanted desperately to help push him to victory, came away cold from fundraising events that were supposed to allow them intimate access to the president.

*New York Times* columnist Maureen Dowd captured the contrast memorably:

> He [Obama] rationed his smile, his eloquence and his electricity, playing the dispassionate observer, delegating, dithering and rushing in at the last moment to try to save the day. A cold shower to Bill's warm bath … .

Obama appears to be a man who believed he could change American politics and culture merely by offering impressive purple prose and by convening reasonable adults around the table to be, well, reasonable. He was destined to struggle for that reason.

Historians may well conclude that Obama won re-election in no small part because Clinton tirelessly used his Disraeli-esque ability to reconnect donors, the Democratic base and independent voters to an Obama who couldn't make the connection on his own.

**Agreeing to Disagree**

Depending on your politics, you may quibble sharply with my preceding observations about Obama and the Clintons, especially if I may be getting close to that uncomfortable area of judging one of them as better than the other as a leader or as a person. That would be fair and understandable. My point is hardly to offer an irrefutable assessment of them, but rather to help us break down and study that complicated blend of traits that various leaders display, in order to better understand where a leader may be able to improve.

**A Farewell to Statues**

A statue is a dead thing; a Disraeli-style leader helps bring others alive.

Lao Tzu spoke thousands of years ago about how a good leader is one who is loved by the people, followed by the one who is feared, and, worst of all, the one who is despised.

Yet the best leader, he shockingly argued, is one who is barely noticed; such that, when her work is done, the people say, "Just look at what we did ourselves!"

That is the same as Jim Collins Level 5 leadership (mentioned in Chapter 4), in which a driven yet low-ego leader is able to take an organization from good to great by being the antithesis of the celebrity leader.

**Moving from Great Monologues to Great Conversations**

In our democratized social media times, people aren't nearly as eager to sit back as an observer of a monologue as they are to engage in a real conversation. The Gladstonian leader thus risks extinction, or at least marginalization, in this era. He may be the management equivalent of the tormented, little-known artist who walks around all day puzzled by how his genius lacks an adequate audience.

In some ways, this takes pressure off a leader. She no longer feels the obligation to be the smartest person in the room every moment of the day. Her premier role is rather to call upon and draw out the genius of others. The leader of today's (and, without much doubt, tomorrow's) new context will be curators of the talents of others.

Having a Disraelian eye for genius involves a certain humility on the part of the manager, because otherwise she will constantly be one-upping subordinates who make the mistake of letting their light shine forth.

Then having that eye also involves a certain detachment. If you are too close to a person, you will become too intimate with their shortcomings through various encounters, competitions, conflicts and over-familiarity.

Mark Twain's mother had the Disraelian touch. Perhaps that is why, in his autobiography, he was able to make one of the most striking observations I've seen about discovering genius in others:

> A genius is not very likely to ever discover himself; neither is he very likely to be discovered by his intimates. ... St. Peter's cannot be impressive for size to a person who has always seen it close at hand and has never been outside of Rome; it is only the stranger, approaching from far away in the Campagna, who sees Rome as an indistinct and characterless blur, with the mighty cathedral standing up out of it all lonely and unfellowed in its majesty. Thousands of geniuses live and die undiscovered—either by themselves or by others.

The last line quoted is tragic. Thousands of geniuses live and die undiscovered. It may even be said that most everyone has some aspect of the genius in him or her. But unless it is drawn out by others, it will remain dormant.

Here the Gladstonian becomes an outright menace to humanity's highest aspirations. Rather than draw out the richest aspects of each person in her charge, she competes for oxygen in the room, so at evening's end she is inevitably the most impressive person in the minds of others.

Such a leader, who needs to constantly assert her omniscience and achieve some sort of immortality, will more often than not sabotage subordinates who dare question her authority or who, worse yet, meet her authority with superior ideas of their own.

## Questions for the CEO Interview

Directors on corporate and nonprofit boards have some of the most important jobs in human organizational life.

Even though the president or CEO of an organization is conventionally viewed as the all-powerful head of the organization, the directors and board members typically hold true responsibility for the life of their institution. The CEO administers, but the board governs. The CEO may offer a vision and seek to implement it, but it is the board that has responsibility for affirming that vision and assessing the CEO's ability to realize it.

Yet because the conventional Lone Hero view of leadership is so pervasive (even among board members themselves), boards typically look for an impressive and imposing Gladstone-style figure, give him all practical authority and leave till the next meeting, at which they rubber-stamp various decisions made by the imposing leader.

If you are a board member, for Chevron or Apple or Duke University or the Red Cross or various other types of organizations, imagine using an interview with a prospective CEO as an opportunity to discern whether she is a Gladstonian or Disraelian.

Certain questions help suss the distinction out:

- Tell us about a time when a subordinate showed you a better way of getting to where you wanted your organization to go.
- What do you see as the relationship between the CEO and her leadership team?
- What kinds of lieutenants do you look for when building a leadership team?
- Tell us about the career trajectories of people who've worked under you.

The Gladstone-style leader often may have some similarities or overlaps with the Compass-Driven Leader examined in Chapter 3. And having a strong compass is essential to being an effective leader.

The Disraelian leader is superior only if we assume that he has a sufficiently strong compass of his own. It need not be as strong as that of the Gladstone-style leader (in fact, we would prefer that it isn't as strong!), but it needs be strong enough to not be talked into any scheme by his most eloquent or determined executives.

Let's return to the issue of statues, from a theological perspective.

Moses' Second Commandment declared, "Thou shalt craft no images, whether in the form of anything in heaven or on earth or in the water."

That intense divine counsel has been pretty much disregarded since the beginning because most people believe that the commandment's intent was to ban idolatry, not photography. In our day, most everything is about images. And as Neil Postman noted in *Amusing Ourselves to Death: Public Discourse in the Age of Show Business*, televised images in particular have rewired how we see our world.

But throughout the ages, a few odd folks have taken the prohibition of images more seriously. Zealous Protestant reformers in Europe eagerly smashed the icons and images of the Roman Catholic Church. Taliban members smashed Buddhist icons in Afghanistan despite an international outcry to preserve ancient cultural artifacts. Mujahideen fighting the Soviets in the 1980s banned grave markers that would commemorate their own dead.

The profound psychological reason for this odd and uptight behavior is the sense that to see a representational image is to naturally venerate it. A god who is invisible risks losing market share to a god who is able to sit on your mantle.

We do tend to have an inflated view of whatever we see depicted in art and craft. This occurred to me when I happened to see a large, framed picture of the produce manager at the local grocery store, discussing in fine detail his commitment to only the freshest and finest fruits and vegetables.

Just then, the man passed by. I paused and thought, "It's him! It's the famous produce manager I've been reading about!"

At that point, it occurred to me how something so trivial had become, for about a nanosecond, exciting to me. I began to reflect on the Paris Hilton effect, whereby Paris Hilton (for about 15 and 1/2 minutes) accumulated undeserved fame through previously undeserved fame. It's why most celebrities seem to take on a power that they do not inherently have, simply because people have become accustomed to seeing their faces in prominent places.

## It Takes Two to Get Tangled

Due to an excess of narcissism, many (perhaps most) aspiring leaders spend more time aspiring to have a statue erected of themselves than aspiring to benefit an organization, a cause or a society. They spend more time aspiring to seem god-like than aspiring to take people in a new direction, hence more addicted to the attention than the obligations they take on.

Followers, in turn, fuel the leader's addiction. People seem to magnetically fall in love with certain leaders, idealizing them and idolizing them. (Charm or beauty need not be the leader's primary asset—few people enjoyed a greater cult of personality among their followers than former Penn State football Coach Joe Paterno, and he was no cover model.)

No one can agree on why followers tend to idolize leaders. Some theorize that societies that have a monotheistic tradition will also have a tendency to place one mighty man or woman in a lordship role. Others theorize that it is an evolutionary vestige of a pre-human tendency to defer to an alpha figure, just as wolves and other animals do. And other theories abound.

Followers inevitably tire of an exalted leader, however, at least until he goes away for a long time and allow for a wave of nostalgia to rise. Ronald Reagan may have roads and airports named after him now, but the talk in his final two years was of "Reagan fatigue" and an extended lame-duck role. Reagan himself protested, "I reject a potted plant presidency," which did not have the desired effect of reasserting himself at the center of national and world events.

Ralph Waldo Emerson said it best: "Every hero at last becomes a bore." This is why, if you're a board member, you don't do well to seek out a Statue Leader to run your business. If you're a stakeholder, you don't do well to encourage a cult of personality. And even (or especially) if you're a leader or aspiring leader yourself, you don't do well to tolerate your own vanities too easily. At some point, power and influence ebb.

The tendency to worship heroes and leaders is out of step with the democratic system that has largely won the day. Going the Disraelian way, not the Gladstonian way, is the best way to go.

## Generation 'N'

Ours is said to be an increasingly narcissistic society. Christopher Lasch wrote of the phenomenon two decades ago in *The Culture of Narcissism,* and Drew Pinksy examined it at length more recently in *The Mirror Effect: How Celebrity Narcissism is Seducing America.*

Social media technologies, reality television and overly protective modern parenting styles are often pointed to as factors. There is also substantial evidence that narcissistic disorders have ticked up a few percentage points in the larger society—which means that it has increased substantially among the younger population, which has been most shaped by such factors.

To those with such a mindset, the Disraelian way will seem difficult, even alien. Accustomed as they are to being the apples of their parents' eyes and to winning large trophies for minor participation, they will struggle to understand why they don't have a Gladstonian effect on the world once they are in a less nurturing environment than their own home.

My own observation is that the millennial generation, which is sometimes known as the Lost Generation (due to the economic stagnation that they've inherited) or the Entitled Generation (due to the spoiling done by helicopter parents) could better be called the 10 Percent Generation. That is because only about 10 percent of them are naturally suited to the manner of workplace culture and office politics instituted by the women and men who will be their superiors for the next 20 years. Those who can drop any Gladstonian pretenses and shift to the Disraelian way will have a substantial competitive edge.

# SEVEN

## YOU NEVER CAN SAY GOODBYE

**THE ROAD TO HELL:** Julius Caesar was loved by the people, and he used his power and popularity to make himself dictator for life. Sixty members of the Senate thought better of it. And Caesar fast went from a living legend to a dead one. Because the people loved this vain but gracious and skilled emperor, a messy civil war resulted, the sort not seen again until Joe Paterno's statue was removed from the Penn State campus.

**THE ROAD OUT OF HELL:** The ancient Roman citizen Cincinnatus was twice summoned from his farm, to go to the halls of power and wield absolute authority. Twice, he immediately handed the rod of power back and went home to the farm after he had completed his appointed task.

Consider again some foundational themes of this book.

- Most leaders and would-be leaders have an unbalanced ego; some have too little, and, well, most have too much.
- Most of these people are unhappy.
- Most of these people are less effective and less successful than they could be.

Of course, many unhappy and not-entirely successful people tend to become highly admired anyway. This is especially the case if they have both excess ego and a good share of charisma. Given the many ways in which narcissists cultivate their charms from an early age in their quest for adoration, you can be certain that a fair number of charismatic egotists will have their entire identity intertwined with their leadership positions.

At some point, however, power and authority ebb—for even the most charismatic leader as well as the most imposing Statue Leader. It becomes, like for Cincinnatus, time to go home to the farm.

Yet a large number of leaders, who were predisposed toward excessive egotism in the first place, grow outright addicted to the level of authority that they enjoyed at their peak. Then when they begin to suspect that that their authority has indeed ebbed, they double down on their commitment to command undiluted authority. They may not even realize it, but they fear that they would be a non-entity if they were surgically removed from their job.

They thus fail at one of the most essential aspects of leadership—the smooth and effective hand-off of power and authority to others.

Remember Lao Tzu's words: "When the work is done, and one's name is becoming distinguished, to withdraw into obscurity is the way of Heaven." But the Statue Leader cannot withdraw into obscurity and deceives himself into believing that the only path to serenity is to try, quite literally *in vain*, to recreate old magic.

Tzu's words again are instructive: "Those who possessed in highest degree the attributes of the way of Heaven did not seek to show them, and therefore they possessed them in fullest measure. Those who possessed in a lower degree those attributes sought how not to lose them, and therefore they did not possess them in fullest measure."

So too are the words of Cato the Elder: "After I am dead, I would rather have man ask why Cato has no monument than why he has one."

If a leader is on the decline, as most leaders will be at some point, the ability to emulate Mark Twain's ailing but outwardly-focused mother becomes crucial to minimizing narcissistic overreaching. Recall Twain's words about how "the invalid who takes a strenuous and indestructible interest in everything and everybody but himself, and to whom a dull moment is an unknown thing and an impossibility, is a formidable adversary for disease and a hard invalid to vanquish."

The other option—the road more traveled—is to allow the leadership addiction to enmesh oneself and one's entire organization in a toxic pathology.

In referring to addiction, I'm being matter-of-fact rather than dramatic. One of the hallmarks of addiction is that the subject gains less pleasure from what he desires than you or he would expect.

Tom Stafford, a cognitive scientist at the University of Sheffield, wrote in a BBC blog:

> [I]n addiction, the theory goes, the circuits can become uncoupled, so that you get extreme wanting without a corresponding increase in pleasure. Matching this, addicts are notable for enjoying the thing they are addicted to *less* than non-addicts. This is the opposite of most activities, where people who do the most are also the ones who enjoy it the most.

This is one curse of Statue leadership: If you have success at it, you might not make it home. You'll be tempted to stay out too long, until disaster strikes or you lose your edge.

Most of us have a certain healthy fear of the debilitating, life-destroying addictions that result from the use of cocaine, heroin and other illegal substances. Most of us recognize that, if we were to casually try such a substance, we would soon find ourselves swirling down a vortex without the ability to find our moorings.

Power is different, perhaps even more treacherous.

No one craves cocaine or heroin without first having tried it; they casually or even accidentally sample it, and only then find the addiction kicking in. But with power and authority, the craving can burn long before the first experience. The first experience rewards the desire, and then it intensifies that desire.

Yet as addiction experts like Stafford note, even as the desire grows more intense, within an addiction, the enjoyment dissipates.

What does this mean? It means several things, for the leader and for her followers and for the stakeholders and members of her governing board.

- You should have a very good reason for staying on in a top leadership role that you've already performed for a long time. Otherwise you may be kidding yourself about your motives and your ability to contribute.
- A wise governing board would ask its president or CEO to re-interview for her position every five years, even if things are going well. This should be an aggressive and unsentimental interview about vision, future goals, organizational weaknesses and succession planning. Wise board members would help the CEO consider ways he can help the organization or the community after stepping down.
- This applies not just for CEOs, but for high-ranking lieutenants too. Some will settle into

a comfortable, high-paying role and stay there without carefully factoring the organization's need for a fresh flow of talent and ideas.

## But What's Next?

There comes a point when a person who's been in a job for many years will (maybe even just subconsciously) reach for the cruise control on the organizational steering wheel. He may show up later at the office than before; he may put less energy or imagination or boldness into thinking of new ventures.

This cutting back may be laudable from the perspective of work-life balance, but if his is a high-achieving organization, and if he has helped make it such an organization, then he may be doing it a disservice by staying in the role after his passion or single-mindedness has ebbed.

In our jumpy (and litigious) times, let me just add that this is not a function of age. A college student who's been in a leadership role more than two years in a row may be as subject to this issue as a corporate executive or a congressperson.

Anyone can run into this problem. In management roles, as in personal relationships, it is hard to pinpoint the difference between knowing the right time to go and giving up.

**We need to be able to ask ourselves if we are still passionate about what we are doing or whether we're there because we don't know where else to be.** (And to make it even harder, we need to be honest with our answer.)

## How Do You Know When It's Time Go?

Let's go back to Square One: If you're a long-established, longtime leader, you need to consult a range of other people to suss out whether you're still as crucial to the organization as you probably think you are. Go back to Chapter 1 and consider whether you're a managerial Babe Ruth who's no longer hitting home runs in the eyes of other people.

## The Rise and Fall of the Roman Emperor

Julius Caesar was beloved and practically worshipped in his own time. Being practically worshipped would not be enough. He became the first living Roman leader to see coins minted with his image and statues that depicted him as more than human—as a figure with outright divine attributes.

Caesar was 56 years old when he was effectively the king of the world. Historian Adrian Goldsworthy notes that, though Caesar had some struggles with epilepsy, he easily could have lived another 15 or 20 years.

Goldsworthy writes in *Caesar: Life of a Colossus*, "As a person Cicero and most other senators still found him [Caesar] pleasant, and his behaviour was moderate and inclined to be generous. It was not so much Caesar the man they hated, but the position that he had acquired and what it meant for the republic."

The Roman republic in fact had the occasional dictator. Those dictatorships were usually limited, six-month terms. Yet toward the end of his life, Caesar accumulated "dictator in perpetuity" powers. Goldsworthy notes that Caesar was coy about such honors, testing with a veneer of false humility to see if there was enough popular support for his rise to ultimate and enduring authority.

Not long after he became the de facto emperor, 60 senators decided enough was enough. They plotted the Ides of March assassination, which was seen as "sudden and unanticipated by all but the conspirators," Goldsworthy writes.

It is said that assassination is the ultimate form of censorship, and the people rioted in protest against the aristocrats who chose unilaterally to censor their leader. Yet far from removing a threat to the republic, the assassins ended up paving the way for the imminent destruction of it. A catastrophic civil war ensued; Caesar's adopted son Octavian (later Augustus) would succeed him, and the republic would be no more.

Yet do those senators deserve the ultimate blame for the fall of the republic and the fall of Caesar? It can be argued that Caesar placed himself and his beloved nation in harm's way.

Contrast his example with that of Cincinnatus.

## Going Home to the Farm

Cincinnatus was the rarest of specimens: a man who had absolute power and the character to relinquish it.

He was a Roman ex-consul, living four and a half centuries before Caesar, who had retired to a small farm, where he spent long days working his fields. While plowing his fields one day, he was greeted by a Roman delegation informing him that he had been elected dictator to help Rome through a battle against the Aequi people. He obeyed, then went back to the farm as soon as he could, refusing the prerogatives of power for even one day longer than necessary.

Two decades later, he was called on again, to address a food-distribution crisis. Again, he went home as soon as he'd solved the crisis.

*Twice* Cincinnatus was called away from the farm to serve as dictator. *Twice* he handed power back early and returned to his farm after he was done with what he needed to do.

"Do your work, then step back," Lao Tzu said in the fifth or sixth century B.C. At roughly the same time he was preaching it, Cincinnatus was embodying it.*

*As an aside, Lao Tzu's historicity can be called into question in the same way that Homer's can. Both may be composites or amalgams of old traditions.*

## The American Cincinnatus

The Roman republic, despite the model of figures such as Cincinnatus, was drained of its democratic lifeblood, in no small part thanks to Caesar. Democracy would not be resurrected until modern times, in no small part because an ambitious man named George Washington chose to take a restrained approach much like that of Cincinnatus.

Washington is a peculiar historical figure—he seems sanitized by the waters of time, to the point that he may be the most revered yet also the most sterile and "boring" of great leaders.

This obscures what truly allowed him to have the greatest legacy in American history.

Twice, Washington had the opportunity to seize absolute power of the nascent American nation. Twice, Washington (like Cincinnatus) resisted that power and returned to his own farm, to Mount Vernon.

It can't be said that Washington was a natural candidate to walk away from absolute power. Historian Garry Wills, in *Certain Trumpets: The Nature of Leadership*, noted that Washington early on displayed a charisma and forcefulness that made him a natural leader; and he added to this a flair for the theatrics of leadership, right down to designing for himself special uniforms to dazzle the troops and the masses.

Wills went so far as to say that, "though George Washington rose from dim origins, nothing was more wildly improbable than his return to a quiet private station at the end of a dizzying career."

Yet the ambitious Washington began his career as "a world-famous bungler," in the words of the historian. His colonial militia attacked a French diplomatic delegation in 1754, setting off a major conflict between Europe's greatest powers. Washington was censured by King George II, he resigned his commission, and "his wounded pride took years of salving, and the preservation of his dignity became an overriding concern," Wills writes.

It's against this backdrop that Washington's actions toward the end of his life become so extraordinary. After the long and difficult revolution, he could have seen himself as having earned the right to serve as dictator. Most Americans would have been pleased with the development; after all, the best working model that anyone at the time knew was a benign and effective constitutional monarchy, and Washington seemed to have the character and constitution to play such a role.

Yet the general, who had been so humiliated by the English early in his career, relinquished his military command after defeating the English and went home. This shocked leaders across the Atlantic, including King George III, who said that only the greatest of men could walk away from absolute power at that point.

After being summoned and begged again to lead a new nation, he consented for a season. He helped develop a new democratic constitution and agreed to be elected for one term of service as president. He was then pressured to serve an extra term. But he resisted the clamor for him to serve more than two terms as president, and with that he helped create an environment in which a democratic nation became bigger than any one person, even its "father."

As someone who understood the theatrics of power, he shrewdly began to "replace his own glamour with the more impersonal symbols of power—the Constitution, the flag, the offices of government, the courts," Wills notes.

Why did Washington step away from power? How could he summon the humility to walk away from a role that he knew he was worthy of?

St. Paul, in his famous passage in Philippians 2, says that Jesus did not cling to his power and divinity, but humbled himself in the form of a mortal. That insinuates that it, quite paradoxically, takes divine power to step away from power.

Wills might agree: "If we look at other revolutionary leaders, from Caesar to Cromwell to Napoleon, we have to conclude that it is even harder to give up power than to acquire it."

Yet Washington was not divine, not even necessarily "inspired." Yes, Washington was guided by some lofty ideals and principles.

But remember that Washington "bungled" his reputation early in his career and spent many years reflecting on how to repair it and cement it. Ultimately, Washington appears to have been a pragmatist who, having repaired that reputation through years of strife and peril, was determined that his own vanity would not stain that reputation.

Wills wrote:

> "He wielded power by yielding it. His fame spread through Europe as the new Cincinnatus, the ancient Roman who left his army to return to his farm. His reputation, the dearest thing to him,

was bound up in service. To seize power, in any way that hurt his reputation would be felt as the greatest defeat by Washington."

It took brilliant Enlightenment visionaries such as Thomas Jefferson and James Madison and Benjamin Franklin and Alexander Hamilton to conceive democracy for a modern era. But it took Washington to birth it—and he did so by knowing, more than almost anyone in history, when it was time to go home.

Now you have to admit: Washington is not as boring as you thought, is he? The man's greatness went immeasurably beyond what may have happened surrounding a legendary cherry tree.

At the more depressing end of the Cincinnatus-Caesar spectrum, we find Pervez Musharraf of my own homeland, Pakistan.

Pakistan during Musharraf's tenure, in the first decade of this century, was considered on the verge of becoming a failed state. Foreign affairs observers argued that it wasn't too big to fail, but was too important to fail. It was the Muslim world's second most populous country, and the only one with nuclear weapons. It was the descendant of the rich and proud Indus Valley civilizations. Its location was of great strategic importance to the West, whether during the Soviet occupation of neighboring Afghanistan or during the American campaign against the Taliban, Al Qaeda and other extremists.

Musharraf was a talented and charismatic leader, and his own success seemed essential to officials in Washington and across the West. He was a religious moderate in a nation that had become infected with religious fundamentalism. And he was willing to be a close ally of Washington in the war on terror, even though this resulted in multiple attempts on his life by Islamic extremists.

Musharraf, previously the head of his nation's military, did not come to power through normal democratic means but through a bloodless coup. In 1999, he deposed Prime Minister Nawaz Sharif, whose corrupt government had lost credibility and legitimacy (Pakistan had a history of generals, in the name of stability, who tossed out civilian governments that were struggling).

The general (now president) pledged to return the country to democracy. Critics rolled their eyes.

Yet temporary dictatorship in times of crisis has been a fact of life, and not just in the time of Rome. Critics of Abraham Lincoln complained that his own efforts to suspend the writ of habeus corpus smacked of tyranny, while his supporters called such efforts temporary necessities.

Many called for a temporary dictator to guide America through the Great Depression. When Franklin D. Roosevelt took office in 1933, William Randolph Hearst even released a fictional film account of an American strongman to help ease the American public into accepting a season of dictatorship.

That became Musharraf's own ambition. He held, and won, a reasonably legitimate election in 2002, though he re-engineered the government to be a loose hybrid between dictatorship.

I wrote a newspaper column in 2005 pleading for Musharraf to play the Cincinnatus role if democracy was to take deep root in Pakistan. I argued that he needed to step down rather than continually cling to his position.

He obviously didn't read or heed the *Ashland Daily Tidings*. As new elections approached in 2007, Musharraf announced that he intended to remain in power for five more years—despite polls showing two-thirds of his citizens wanted him gone and despite opposition from other branches of government. He also struggled on the international front: He sought to maintain his alliance with a wary U.S. government even as he knew that some elements of Pakistan's own army and intelligence agencies were in cahoots with the extremists that the U.S. was fighting. His standing at home continued to crumble.

Musharraf insisted that his own country and its allies would in time come to appreciate his sacrifice on their behalf. But reality wouldn't bend to his will as much as he liked.

Musharraf continued that Pakistan wasn't yet ready for a lighter democratic touch. He may have been right. But where Washington gained power by yielding power, to use Wills' phrase, Musharraf clung to power and inevitably lost power.

With the advice of Washington (the dysfunctional city, not the wise leader), he cynically invited back to Pakistan the former Prime Minister Benazir Bhutto, who had been exiled after twice being removed from office for corruption. (Bhutto, revered in the West as a progressive leader, was herself an antithesis of Cincinnatus.)

I believe Musharraf sincerely wanted to help his country, but he also needed to retain supremacy, because he convinced himself he was essential to his country's salvation.

This approach is not surprising. The gene that makes a person the kind of alpha dog who leads others is the same gene that makes a person cling to a leadership role after he's no longer welcome.

Finally, Musharraf had to choose between resigning in disgrace or being impeached in parliament. It could be in doubt whether he was being handled wisely or justly—but as with Caesar, catastrophe wouldn't have struck if he focused more on succession and less on personal success.

Could it possibly have been enjoyable for Musharraf to hold power? Of course not. He knew his life was in danger as president. He knew more assassinations would come. Perhaps his drive could only be explained by the addiction that comes from top leadership.

While Musharraf found himself pushed into the sort of political and geographic exile that Bhutto had suffered, Bhutto herself would tragically be assassinated in the free-for-all that Pakistani politics became. The country labored through worse political chaos than ever.

Musharraf wasn't done yet. He would posture as if to find a way to be welcomed back triumphantly. In 2013 he returned from exile, claiming to be on a mission "to save Pakistan." Few noticed or cared.

The lesson is simple. America had a Cincinnatus; Pakistan needed one but did not have one. That Musharraf had the potential to play that role, but could not do so, has had a damaging effect on global affairs to this day.

Legendary college basketball coach John Wooden was a Cincinnatus in his realm, in a way that college football coach Joe Paterno wasn't able to be—and the consequences were cosmic.

Both coaches had long and admirable tenures.

Over 27 years at the helm of UCLA, Wooden won 10 national titles, more than any other college basketball coach. Wooden had spent 16 years with modest success in Westwood before perfecting his system and winning his first national championship banner in 1964. The titles came in a cascade after that—nine more in the next 11 years.

He announced his retirement in 1976, at the age of 64, knowing that he had nothing left to *prove*, and that he could find other ways to *express* himself. He had decades of wisdom and life in him at that point; he would spend some of that time enjoying his family and grandchildren, some of that time mourning the loss in 1985 of his beloved wife, Nell, and some of that time simply reading and studying quietly.

Later he would increasingly write books and give lectures and mentor new generations of coaches and players around the nation. At UCLA, he had a designated seat from which he would watch and encourage his successors on the UCLA bench. While many UCLA fans wished he had remained on the bench himself, he believed it was better for everyone that he allow the next generation of coaches and players to find their way, even while he generously made himself available as a mentor and guide.

Over 46 years as Penn State's head coach, Paterno won 409 games, more than any other college football coach. He was revered for demanding that his players go to class, graduate, follow the rules and become honorable men.

At the age of 65 in 1992, Paterno was going strong, and he chose to keep going. At the age of 73, he found his team struggling, and he found columnists and critics speculating that he'd lost his edge and that the game had passed him by.

Paterno's response was defiant. He buckled down and insisted he would return Penn State to prominence. He eventually did, with a successful season in 2005.

Yet even then he couldn't go out on top and he seemed to lose control of the team. A few years later, an ESPN story would report: "Since 2002, 46 Penn State football players have faced 163 criminal charges, according to an ESPN analysis of Pennsylvania court records and reports. Twenty-seven players have been convicted of or have pleaded guilty to a combined 45 counts."

Had Paterno retired when he should have, in perhaps the mid-1990s, he would be viewed in a completely different light. Paterno's vanity kept him from retiring, to the point that he had become a national joke even before scandal arose, as *The Onion* mock-reported that Penn State players were all worried that they would be the one to accidentally land on and kill their frail coach.

Then came allegations in 2011 that he either turned a blind eye during the past several decades to the pedophilia of longtime assistant Jerry Sandusky, or, more sinisterly, actively worked to keep Sandusky's crimes off the public radar.

Quite telling are the recent words of columnist David Jones:

> In covering the man and his football program for 21 seasons, the single most dominant thread is this: his ambition and drive...He could be a vindictive man. At times, he was pointlessly petty and nasty.
>
> Just like the rest of us. Except that in the case of a man who had accumulated such power, the consequences of his actions could take on much greater impact.

As any Penn State alum will tell you, Joe Pa did enormous good for his school and his community. He gave generously, he lived modestly, and he made damned sure that generations of football players got degrees and moved into respectable careers.

But as most non-Penn-Staters will tell you, he seemed to put the image of his legacy above a rigorous commitment to rooting out monsters. That intuition seems now to be confirmed reality, based on the findings of an investigation led by former FBI head Louis Freeh.

Paterno refused to retire several years before the scandal, even when asked by his superiors. In this way, he showed a *l'etat, c'est moi* attitude that gives birth to so much corruption and abuse, indirectly if not directly.

Peter Robb, writing about the mafia in *Midnight in Sicily*, made the following observation:

> The old mafia reward hadn't been wealth but power. 'Giving orders is better than fucking,' was an often-heard mafia saying.

And so it is for leaders.
But there is a better way.

If a leader is on the decline, as all leaders will be at some point, the ability to emulate Mark Twain's ailing mother becomes crucial to avoiding narcissistic or even sociopathic overreaching. Recall Twain's words about how "The invalid who takes a strenuous and indestructible interest in everything and everybody but himself, and to whom a dull moment is an unknown thing and an impossibility, is a formidable adversary for disease and a hard invalid to vanquish."

Leaving behind a role of power need not be death, not even for the alpha leader. There are many meaningful—and even high profile—ways to serve. The added blessing is that she can now make a contribution while being *liberated* from some of the most odious and tedious aspects of leadership.

- The leader can become a mentor. Indeed, this may well be the most crucial and necessary role that a successful leader can assume.
- The leader can become a face for his organization, without worrying about many of the headaches. Eric Schmidt stepped down from his CEO role at

Google in 2011, at the age of 55, yet assumed the chairman's role, which was a far more ceremonial position. That gave him the ability to stay active while simultaneously allowing co-founder Larry Page to finally move from an understudy role into the top spot.
- The leader can teach. Or write. Or both. Bill George is a former chairman and chief executive officer of Medtronic. After stepping down as chairman of Medtronic's board in 2002, he began a new career at Harvard Business School, teaching and writing four bestselling leadership books.
- The leader can give back. Thousands of worthy non-profits need successful leaders and ex-leaders on their boards, to serve as advocates and ambassadors. Max Depree, the widely admired CEO of the Herman Miller office furniture company, served after retirement as the chairman of the board of trustees of Fuller Theological Seminary. In that role, he brought his experience and wisdom to bear on issues facing an organization and cause that he cared about deeply.

# EPILOGUE

## ICARUS FELL. NO ONE NOTICED.

Led Zeppelin was such a masterfully talented rock band, with such a menacing mystique, that some wondered whether they'd made a pact with the devil for their fame. The band simultaneously seemed to resist yet playfully embraced such imagery.

The picture on their Swan Song record label depicted a glorious winged being who appeared to be falling, and observers took turns guessing whether the being was Lucifer falling from heaven, Icarus falling after attempting to get too close to the sun, or the sun god Apollo descending at dusk.

Icarus presents a fascinating nuance to the notion that leadership can be a Faustian bargain.

According to the Icarus legend: Boy is warned not to fly too close to the sun, boy vainly heads straight for the sun, boy's wings fail, and the cocky brat scorches his wings and falls.

While there tends to be some variation in the details based on who's recounting the legend, it's meaningful to look closely at Ovid's telling of the myth: Icarus is the son of Daedalus, and they both are imprisoned on the island of Crete by King Minos. Daedalus decides that the only way to escape the island is by crafting two sets of wings out of feathers and wax. After testing his own wings out with success, he gives Icarus one set—and a key caution:

"Icarus, I recommend thee to keep the middle tract; lest, if thou shouldst go too low, the water should clog thy wings; if too high, the fire of the sun should scorch them. Fly between both."

Most of us think that the only mistake involved flying too high. But as Ovid notes, flying too low would cause disaster too. Leaders must see their own egos in much the way that we see Icarus.

The majority of leaders and aspiring leaders have an excess of ego. Most humans see a podium or a microphone and they flee; the typical aspiring leader sees a podium and sees it as his divinely bestowed inheritance, usually to be shielded from would-be rivals.

On occasion, however, you encounter a person with too little ego, the one who Daedalus warned about, the one who would fly too low and become bogged down. Such a person may feel a longing to take people in new and better directions but may find it hard to actually get them moving. Or such a person may be thrust into a key management position and, without being a natural leader, must begin to grasp and practice the art of moving people in a new direction.

A healthy ego travels between extremes. A healthy ego is an ego that sees clearly, that knows its strengths and limitations, and that lives authentically within the extremes of those strengths and limitations.

Both the underinflated ego and the overinflated ego lack such understanding. Both are typically driven by fear—in the former case a fear of failure and in the latter case a fear of insignificance ("Glory is fleeting, but obscurity is forever," that blowhard Napoleon once remarked).

Do *you* have the right stuff to lead well? You probably recognize by now that it ultimately comes down to whether you have the right amount of ego.

No matter what form of organization or governance we're discussing, ego remains the rocket fuel for leadership.

Too little, and you'll never make it into orbit.

Too much, and you'll pop like a firework in the clouds.

Here's the amazing thing: So many aspiring and practicing leaders live nervous lives, constantly checking the mirror for signs of waxing or waning greatness. Meanwhile, the world goes on.

While the fall of Icarus is seen as one of the great tragic figures of myth and literature, it's helpful to take a peek at Pieter Bruegel's painting, "Landscape with the Fall of Icarus." Two legs are visible, upside-down in the water, as Icarus plunges downward to his doom. The head carried the body down. Yet farmers plow the fields, shepherds tend to their flocks, and a ship sets forth on sail, none of them noticing his state.

The poet W.H. Auden suggested that there was something liberating about the idea that the world keeps turning, paying little mind to our current standing in the rankings of great people.

The 10-year-old who wants to be a leader is like Icarus in many ways, wanting to touch the sun despite the known risks of getting burned. Most people who want to be leaders don't necessarily want to do the hard, even hellish work of leadership; most simply want to be great.

When we consider Bruegel's image, we can begin to see how the typical leader's desperate quest for glory is secondary to the workings of the world. Many of the leaders discussed in these pages got it right. Many got it wrong. But the ones who got it right, and who made an impact, were the ones who had a strong enough sense of self to make things happen — and a willingness to keep that sense of self in proper perspective and proportion.

My hope is that you will be one of those people in the months and years ahead.